Samsung Galaxy Tab® 4 NOOK®

FOR DUMMIES®

A Wiley Brand

by Corey Sandler

FOR DUMMIES®
A Wiley Brand

Samsung Galaxy Tab® 4 NOOK® For Dummies®

Published by: **John Wiley & Sons, Inc.,** 111 River Street, Hoboken, NJ 07030-5774, www.wiley.com

Copyright © 2015 by John Wiley & Sons, Inc., Hoboken, New Jersey

Published simultaneously in Canada

For general information on our other products and services, please contact our Customer Care Department within the U.S. at 877-762-2974, outside the U.S. at 317-572-3993, or fax 317-572-4002. For technical support, please visit www.wiley.com/techsupport.

Wiley publishes in a variety of print and electronic formats and by print-on-demand. Some material included with standard print versions of this book may not be included in e-books or in print-on-demand. If this book refers to media such as a CD or DVD that is not included in the version you purchased, you may download this material at http://booksupport.wiley.com. For more information about Wiley products, visit www.wiley.com.

Library of Congress Control Number: 2014948514

ISBN 978-1-119-00834-7 (pbk); ISBN 978-1-119-00836-1 (ePub); ISBN 978-1-119-00835-4 (ePDF)

Manufactured in the United States of America

10 9 8 7 6 5 4 3 2

Contents at a Glance

Table of Contents

Introduction

· ·

*N*early everything you can do on a desktop or laptop computer can now be accomplished on a small, battery-operated handheld rectangle of plastic and glass. The best way to think of a tablet like the Samsung Galaxy Tab 4 NOOK is as a super-sized smartphone, without the cellular phone connection (and monthly bill).

The tablet isn't the most advanced model on the market — many others have sharper screens or better cameras or other fancy doodads — but for its purpose as an eBook reader and a portal on the Internet — the Samsung Galaxy Tab 4 NOOK is a very good option at a relatively low price.

About This Book

As good as the new NOOK tablet is, they have continued a long tradition in computer manufacturing: The skimpy little instruction manual that comes with it is laughably inadequate and the online booklet isn't much better. Myself, I'm not complaining: I've made a nice living for a long time filling in the gaping blanks between. Herewith, then, the keys to the Galaxy.

You can read this book from front to back, if you wish. Or you can jump to a section that deals with whatever questions you have. Each of the parts deal with a particular task or function, and each chapter covers a specific topic.

My goal, as always, is to present *news you can use* and skip over as much unnecessary bafflegab as possible. When I feel it necessary to go a bit into technological detail, you'll find those sections nicely fenced off; enter if you want, or keep the barn door latched. We're in this together, and I've done my best to make the book easy to read and understand, and even entertaining in places.

The full name of the device we're gathered to explore is the Samsung Galaxy Tab 4 NOOK. It's very much a member of the Samsung Galaxy Tab family, in its fourth generation. But that last word, NOOK, means that some important parts of the operating system and reading apps are different from its cousins.

I'll call the tablet by its first name when it seems appropriate, and in other places I call it the Tab 4 NOOK. And in places where the hardware is not the issue, I might even just call it the NOOK or the tablet. We'll see, together.

Like other books in the constantly expanding *For Dummies* universe, you'll be directed to do things by numbered steps. Sometimes you'll be advised to *choose* a menu item, and then to *tap* a command. It's all quite touchy-feely, I promise.

Foolish Assumptions

The first and most important assumption I make for all of my books of this sort is this: **You, dear reader, are an intelligent, capable, and curious person who wants to know how to *use* what seems at first glance to be a very complex technical device.**

Put another way, you're not looking to build a Samsung Galaxy Tab 4 NOOK from spare parts recovered from your kitchen junk drawer, and you have no interest whatsoever in writing your own software to make the hardware sing and dance.

And the second assumption is this: **You already own, or are seriously considering buying, a Tab 4 NOOK.**

And because we're more than halfway through the first decade of the tablet computer, I suspect that **you have seen a tablet** and probably made at least a few swipes at one. Because of this, I skip the "Isn't it amazing?" part and get right to the point: They keep getting better and better.

I do believe that there are things that any reader would find interesting and helpful in this book, but to be fully honest about it, this book is pretty tightly focused on just that one model of tablet.

Although it isn't essential, I also assume that **you have your own desktop or laptop computer or have access to one.** It doesn't matter whether it be a Windows or Macintosh design. And I also have to assume that you have a Wi-Fi wireless computer network you can use at home or at work or in a public library or other place you can use; the Tab 4 NOOK needs a Wi-Fi connection to allow you to fill it with books and other media and to reach the Internet.

Another assumption is that **you've heard this relatively new word many, many times: *app.*** It is short for application, which is another word for a software program. On a desktop or laptop computer, software has become larger and more complex year by year. But in the reduced world of the tablet, there's a different concept: small and specialized.

Icons Used in This Book

This icon is there to tell you when danger — or at least serious problems — lie ahead. If you don't heed this information, you might damage your tablet or yourself or you might lose really important information.

This icon is there to remind you of something. This information tells you how to do something you'll often need.

This icon tells you of useful tips and suggestions to get the most from your new tablet. This information might save you time or money. Or better — both.

You probably don't need to know this stuff, but aren't you a little bit curious? Go ahead, try a few. There are no pop quizzes in this book.

Beyond the Book

I've written a lot of extra content that you won't find in this book. Links to the articles are on the parts pages. Go online to find the following:

- **Make a profile for each person who uses your tablet at**

  www.dummies.com/extras/samsunggalaxytabs

- **If you can't automatically connect to an established email server, try Samsung's recommendations at**

  www.dummies.com/extras/samsunggalaxytabs

- **Get the best pictures possible from the camera with help from**

  www.dummies.com/extras/samsunggalaxytabs

- **Take certain points into consideration before buying an app**

  www.dummies.com/extras/samsunggalaxytabs

- **Find out about ten fun or helpful — and free — apps at**

  www.dummies.com/extras/samsunggalaxytabs

✔ **The Cheat Sheet for this book is at**

> `www.dummies.com/cheatsheet/samsunggalaxytabs`

Here you'll find instructions for taking a panoramic picture, finding images online, make a slide show, using SoundAlive, and replacing regular alarm sounds with a song.

✔ **Updates to this book, if we have any, are at**

> `www.dummies.com/extras/samsunggalaxytabs`

Where to Go from Here

You go from here to the first part and the sections that lie behind. You could start by reading the copyright and trademark page, or read the names of all of the fine people at Wiley who helped transform my keyboard taps into the book you are holding. But perhaps you'd like to save that for an epilogue. Go forth and explore Samsung Galaxy Tab 4 NOOK and the device itself; they're meant for each other.

Part I

Getting Started with Samsung Galaxy Tab 4 NOOK

getting started

with

Samsung Galaxy Tab 4 NOOK

In this part . . .

- ✔ Explore the Tab 4 NOOK parts.
- ✔ Turn it on and set it up it for first use.
- ✔ Read about how to use the touchscreen.
- ✔ Tap and talk to the keyboard.

1

The First NOOK in the Galaxy

In This Chapter

▶ Figuring out how to turn it on and off

▶ Going into Airplane Mode

▶ Putting memory on a microSD card

You've got a small box that holds a thin, flat piece of plastic and circuitry that has more speed, more intelligence, and more magic than an entire field of mainframes. It can hold and display nearly all of the world's books, magazines, and newspapers. It can sing, show videos, take pictures, make movies, determine its location from an orbiting satellite, connect to the Internet, and send and receive emails and messages.

Just about the only thing the Samsung Galaxy Tab 4 NOOK lacks is a decent instruction manual. If I might be so bold, I'm here to help.

Cozying Up to Your NOOK

To download books (or anything else) or to browse the web with a Tab 4 NOOK, you need access to a Wi-Fi system with an active connection to the Internet. See Figure 1-1.

The small, unpretentious brown cardboard box is about the size of a thick paperback book (remember those?) There's not all that much within: the Galaxy Tab 4 NOOK and some goodies beneath it:

 ✔ **A USB cable:** This cable carries data to and from your tablet when you connect the tablet, via the USB cable, to a laptop or personal computer. The USB cable also lets you recharge the internal battery.

 ✔ **A battery charger:** When you're ready, plug it into an AC wall socket and attach the larger connector of the USB cable to it. Then plug the smaller connector to the Galaxy Tab 4 NOOK. See Figure 1-2.

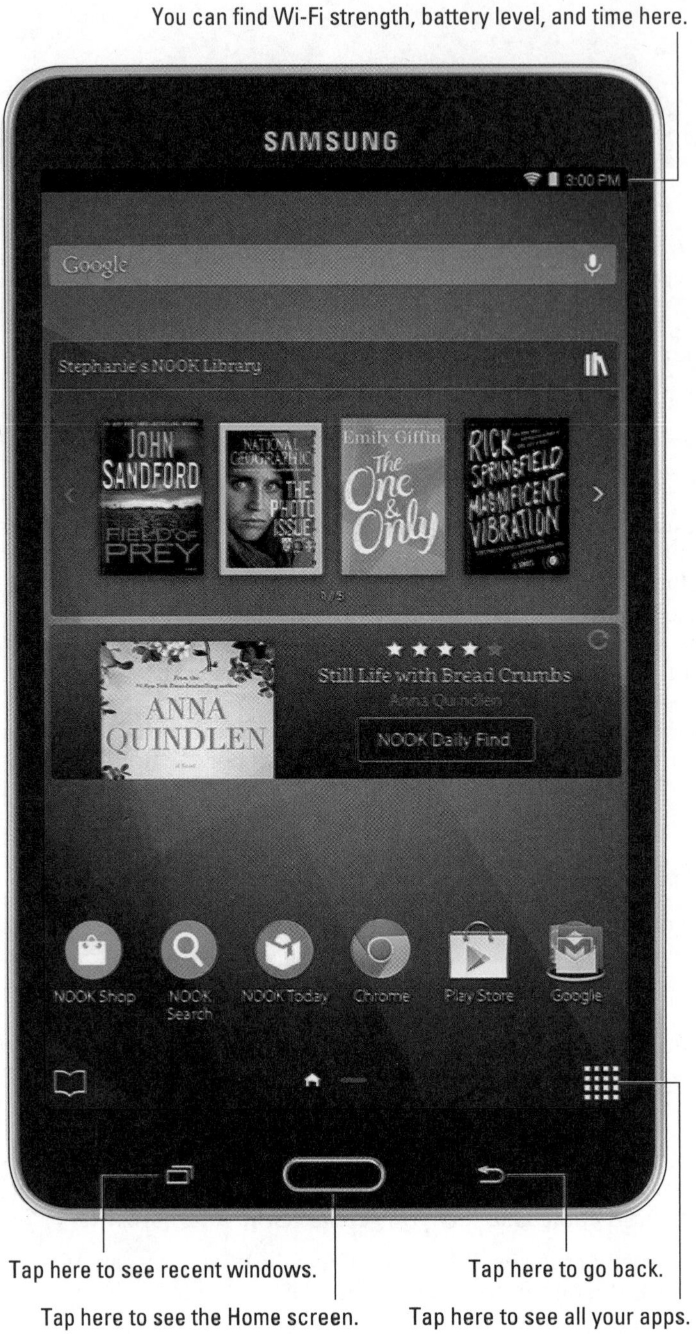

You can find Wi-Fi strength, battery level, and time here.

Tap here to see recent windows.

Tap here to go back.

Tap here to see the Home screen.

Tap here to see all your apps.

Photo courtesy of Barnes & Noble, Inc.

Figure 1-1: Wi-Fi signal strength, battery level, and time are in the upper right. The icon in the lower right displays apps.

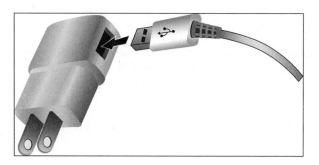

Figure 1-2: The AC adapter plugs into a wall socket; the larger end of the USB cable attaches to the charger.

- ✔ **Two business-card-sized booklets.** One is called the *Health & Safety and Warranty Guide* and it advises you not drop the tablet on your toe, and how if you do Samsung isn't going to pay for the repair. The other booklet, all 20 pages of it (with about six blanks) is called the *Samsung Galaxy Tab 4 NOOK Quick Start Guide*.

Keep the box, along with the warranty information and your receipt. If you need to return the tablet to the seller, send it in for service, or ship it to someone else, the original box is ready to serve and protect.

Sooner or later, you should remove the protective plastic sheet that sits atop the LCD screen. It works well to protect the device in transit, but it will interfere with your use of the touchscreen and collect dirt. Put it back in the box as a memento.

Nothing like Moses's

What's a *tablet?* Way back in ancient times, about 2007 or so, there were laptop computers and the first electronic reading devices, which were single-purpose handheld devices that used something called eInk to draw text on a nearly white background. A few years later the two devices came together in the first successful tablets, which were thin, flat multipurpose computers that used touchscreens instead of keyboards and memory chips instead of spinning hard drives to hold on to data. In 2010, Apple Computer jumped way out front of the pack with the first iPad, and everyone else— Samsung included—has been playing catchup ever since.

Charging the Battery

The Samsung Galaxy Tab 4 NOOK comes with a built-in (and non-removable) rechargeable battery. The battery probably still has some power in it from testing at the factory (mine arrived about half full), but *please resist trying to use it immediately.*

There are three reasons why you want to fully charge the battery before first use:

- ✔ **You want to be assured that the battery, the charger, and the tablet itself are each working properly.**
- ✔ **It may help the battery's longevity.** That is, if you properly *condition* it with a full charge before using it first. See Figure 1-3.

   After the battery is fully charged for the first time, let it drain down to nearly empty, then recharge it fully; do this for the first three or four cycles.

- ✔ **When you first turn on the tablet, you have to register the device with all of its various parts makers.** You have to sign in to a Wi-Fi system with an active Internet connection and sign in with Samsung, Google, a few apps makers, and Barnes & Noble; be sure to install any software updates.

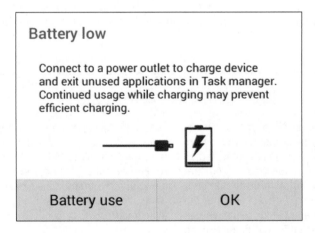

Figure 1-3: The tablet beeps and warns you when the battery level drops to 15 percent. Don't let it drain to 0.

And so, here's how to give your tablet its first full charge:

1. **Attach the larger end of the USB cable to the charger.**

   Pay attention to the black positioning bar inside the charger and its cor-responding bar inside the cable. Don't force the two positioning bars against each other; the cable only fits one way.

2. **Attach the USB cable to the Samsung Galaxy Tab 4 NOOK.**

   The smaller connector on the cable connects to the port on the bottom of the tablet. The side of the cable end that has the three-forked USB symbol will be facing you as you're looking at the front of the tablet. Again, don't force the plug in the wrong way. See Figure 1-4.

3. **Plug the charger into a wall outlet.** Go for a walk, mow the lawn, read a book, bake a cake. For the first three or four times you use your tablet, I recommend draining the battery to near-empty and then fully recharging it.

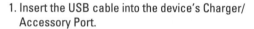

1. Insert the USB cable into the device's Charger/ Accessory Port.

Figure 1-4: The smaller end of the USB cable plugs into the bottom of tablet.

When you plug the charger into a powered-off tablet, the screen will briefly show a battery-like object. You can see roughly how full (or empty) the device is. The drawing disappears after about 15 seconds, and after that there's no way to know the device is being charged: no indicator lights. You'll just have to school yourself to recharge the battery for six or eight hours if it nears empty.

You can recharge your Tab 4 NOOK by connecting the USB cable to a USB port on a PC, although this is a very slow process that takes as many as 10 hours for a full refill. Consider the USB charging option as an emergency backup only.

Inspecting the Gadget

Now for a physical examination. No need for a stethoscope or rubber gloves. Take your Tab 4 NOOK and place it on a desk or table in front of you. See Figure 1-5 for a guided tour of the front of the Samsung Galaxy Tab 4 NOOK. All of the following descriptions are based on looking at the tablet lying on its back, with its top facing away from you and the bottom closest to you: very much like the way you would look at a page from a book.

The front

The front is home to several items of note, one strictly for advertising purposes:

- A Samsung logo at the top of the front
- The front-facing camera lens
- The LCD color touchscreen
- Three keys at the bottom are shown in Figure 1-6. They are, from left to right:
  - *Recent.* Touch and hold it to see apps you've used recently.
  - *Home.* Wherever you are on your tablet, press this key to go to the Home screen.
  - *Back.* Touch to return to the previous screen or option.

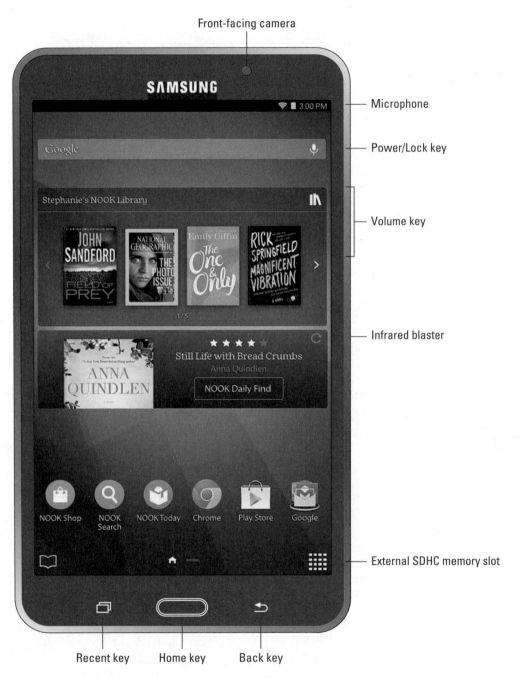

Front-facing camera

Microphone

Power/Lock key

Volume key

Infrared blaster

External SDHC memory slot

Recent key   Home key   Back key

Figure 1-5: A map to the external parts on the front of the Samsung Galaxy Tab 4 NOOK.

Figure 1-6: The keys just below the LCD screen are Recent, Home, and Back.

The left side

Move along. There's nothing to see here, folks. Really. Nothing. The left side of the Galaxy Tab 4 NOOK is so elegantly empty it should go on display at a museum of contemporary art.

The right side

The right side is where you'll find several essential keys, a blaster, a pin-hole, and a slot. Yes, I said *blaster.* From top to bottom on the right side, they are:

- ✔ A tiny hole behind which hides a microphone. It picks up sound for videos, video conferences, and your voice for Internet (not cellular) phone calls. Make sure neither the protective case you use, nor your hand, blocks the opening.

- ✔ The Power/Lock key. Press and hold it for a second or two to turn your Tab 4 NOOK on or off. Press it briefly and release to lock the tablet or wake it from sleep.

- ✔ The Volume key. When the Home screen is displayed, press one end or the other of this rocket key to adjust the volume. When you're playing music, any adjustments you make here affect only music volume. Either way, you know how they work, I'm sure: + means louder and – means quieter, all the way down to mute.

- ✔ The Infrared Blaster. Sorry to have to tell you, but this isn't the latest version of Han Solo's particle beam energy weapon; I'd love to have one to render harmless drivers who cut me off on the expressway. What you have here is an infrared beam that can do things like control your flat-screen TV.

✔ Memory card slot. This tiny opening can accept a little sliver of microSD or microSDHC card that holds information in addition to your tablet's built-in memory. And though 32GB is a whole lot of room, if you fill up one card, you can simply remove it and install a new card.

The top side

Nice and simple, and logically designed: there is but one thing to see here: a headset jack. Here's where you stick a 3.5mm connector for earbuds or connect to an external sound system.

The headset jack works well with earbuds or headphones, but you can also output audio from your Tab 4 NOOK to stereo systems with advanced controls and large speakers. For example, my car has a 3.5mm input jack for its radio; I bought a cable with a 3.5mm plug on each end (called a *male-to-male cable*) to use my NOOK as a music player.

The bottom

There's just one thing to note down here. Although it's lonely, it's actually a very important, multipurpose portal: the microUSB port. Here's where you attach the USB cable that came with your tablet. That cable, in turn, attaches to the AC adapter, allowing you to recharge the internal battery. You can disconnect that same cable from the AC adapter, then connect the cable to a PC or laptop to transfer or sync music or files.

The back

The tablet's back gives the tablet something to hold up the front. To see it, turn your tablet over so that the front is facing down. Although you don't have to baby your device, for safety's sake put a cloth or a magazine under the screen.

Figure 1-7 points out the two items of note are on the back (plus some more advertising and a bit of legalese). Here's what you'll find:

✔ The rear-facing camera. This is your tablet's main camera, for taking photos or videos while you watch the LCD on the other side.

✔ In the lower-right corner is a grill that covers the speaker. If you're going to listen closely to music or speech, don't lay the tablet flat on its back; to get the best sound, you have to make sure the speaker isn't covered.

Rear-facing camera

SAMSUNG

CE0168①X

Speaker

Figure 1-7: The back of the tablet has the rear-facing camera and a tiny speaker.

Turning On, Turning Off, Going to Sleep

The high-tech battery in your Tab 4 NOOK can hold its charge for several weeks when it's young and fresh and the tablet is off. Once you turn it on, the battery should provide power for somewhere between six and ten hours.

You can save battery power by reducing the brightness of the screen and by turning off radios when you don't need them.

Powering on

I imagine you've figured out this is the way to turn on your Samsung Galaxy Tab 4 NOOK: Press and hold the key for two seconds *(one Mississippi, two Mississippi)*.

If this is the first time you've given life to your tablet, you'll immediately start setup, which may take anywhere from 10 to 30 minutes, depending on how much detail you want to get into.

On the other hand, if you've already set up the device, turning it on brings you to either of two places:

- The Home screen (if you haven't required all users to enter a protective pattern, password, or PIN)
- The Lock screen (where have to enter the proper pattern, password, or PIN)

I recommend using the Lock screen and requiring users to enter a code. You'll store personal data, photos, and logins that may keep records of your credit card or banking information.

Powering off

Press the same switch for about two seconds while the device is running. A message asks if you really, really want to do that; tap Power Off to confirm.

Off is off. No alarms will ring, no email will be collected, no music will play.

Why would you want to completely turn off the NOOK tablet?

- You're on an airplane preparing for takeoff or landing and the flight attendant is glaring at you.
- You're in a hospital room with sensitive medical equipment (and doctors).
- You want to put your tablet on the shelf for a month while you sit down with a yellow legal pad to write your own Great American (or Canadian) Novel.

- Your battery is very low and you want to fully recharge it as quickly as possible. Attach the microUSB connector to the tablet and the full-size USB connector to an AC adapter that's plugged into the wall.

Going to sleep

The third option is to put your tablet to sleep, which in electronic terms is *not* the same thing we mean when Fido is headed to the vet for the last time. Putting a tablet to *sleep* means that the LCD screen and most of its internal circuitry are turned off, and just a small amount of power is provided to the system — enough to allow the device to return from the vet, I mean from sleep, at the push of a button. If you put a fully charged NOOK into Sleep mode, it should hold its charge for several days.

Here's how to put the NOOK tablet to sleep: Briefly touch the Power/Lock key. Don't hold it and count river names.

While the tablet's asleep, the following functions are still awake:

- ✔ Email will still be received, *if the Wi-Fi radio is turned on.* You can turn off the Wi-Fi from Settings, or put the tablet into Airplane Mode to reduce power consumption.

- ✔ If your tablet is playing music, that will continue.

- ✔ Any alarms or timers you've set will remain active. (I discuss alarms in Chapter 14.)

To wake up a sleeping NOOK, briefly press the Power/Lock key. If you have required entry of a pattern, password, or PIN, you'll go to the unlock screen; otherwise, the tablet will go directly to the Home screen or the last page you were consulting before its hiatus.

Setting the sleep timeout

Your tablet will go to sleep all by itself if you don't do anything on it for a while. Why would you want this to happen? It'll save battery power and serve as a level of protection if someone lays paws on your NOOK without your permission.

Here's how to customize the sleep control:

1. **Swipe down from the top of the Home screen, and tap the Settings (gear) icon.**

2. **Choose the Device Panel.**

3. **Choose Display.**

4. **Choose Screen Timeout.**

5. **Choose a timeout value from the list.**

   I prefer 5 minutes; the standard value is 30 seconds. You can set the sleep timeout in a range from 15 seconds to one hour.

6. **Press the Home key to return to the Home screen.**

Jetting into Airplane Mode

Although many scientists and some pilots say it's much ado about nothing, most airlines require passengers to turn off all electronic devices during takeoff and landing. The theory was that all of these devices — and by now nearly every passenger has a phone and a tablet and the annoying kid who sat across the row from me on a 12-hour transatlantic flight had a radio-controlled robot — could possibly interfere with an airplane's essential navigational and control systems. Little by little, the airlines and government agencies have been relaxing most of the regulations. In fact, some airlines have begun offering Wi-Fi broadcasts of in-flight movies that can be viewed on tablets, laptops, and phones.

In any case, your nifty NOOK has a setting called Airplane Mode. It disables Wi-Fi and Bluetooth radios but lets you read eBooks and play videos and music.

1. **With two fingers slightly separated, swipe down from the top of the screen.**

   The Quick Panel, a set of shortcuts, appears.

2. **Tap the Airplane Mode icon to turn it on or off.**

   When the feature is on, the airplane icon appears green.

Putting More on a microSD Card

There are enough kinds of *secure digital (SD)* cards to confuse even the experts. There are SD, miniSD, and microSD sizes, and then there are SD, SDHC (high capacity), and SDXC (extended capacity). One example of a microSDHC card is shown in Figure 1-8.

Here's what you need to know about SD cards:

   ✔ *Do* buy a microSD or microSDHC card.

   ✔ *Don't* buy an SD or miniSD card. And don't pay extra for a microSDXC card.

I recommend buying a 16GB or 32GB microSDHC that's class 6 speed. Make sure it's made by a recognized name brand: Kingston, Lexar, Samsung, Sandisk, Toshiba, or Transcend.

Installing a microSDHC card

The kind designers at Samsung have made sure you don't need a post-graduate degree in engineering to install a memory card. You can get to the card slot without removing the back cover; you need no tools other than your fingers.

Figure 1-8: This 32GB microSDHC card is from Kingston Technology.

Just take your time, be careful, and follow these instructions to install a memory card:

1. **Turn off the device.**

   Technically this isn't required, but it is a good practice anytime you're working with electrical devices.

2. **Place your NOOK face up on a well-lit, clean, level surface.**

   Make sure no cups of coffee, soda, water, molten iron, or anything else can spill onto your tablet.

3. **Find the small soft plastic lid on the right side of the tablet.**

4. **Using the tip of your finger, gently pull the lid straight out from the body of the tablet.**

   The lid doesn't completely detach; a flexible band attaches to the lower side. See Figure 1-9.

5. **Hold the memory card *with the printed logo facing up toward you and the small triangle facing toward the Galaxy Tab 4 NOOK. The gold electrical contacts face down, toward the back of the device. Carefully slide it into the slot.***

Figure 1-9: Install a microSDHC with the gold contacts facing away from the front screen and the small triangle marker facing in toward the tablet.

Push gently against the card until it's fully in place. You should hear or feel a click. Don't force it into place; it should fit easily. If it looks about twice as large as the opening, you've got the wrong card. Micros only need apply.

6. **Gently rotate the cover into place and snap it into place.**

When a memory card's installed in the tablet, it is automatically mounted and ready for use. *Mounting* means the tablet has recognized the card.

Mounting a microSDHC card

Here's how to manually mount a memory card that was removed improperly or that somehow isn't automatically mounted by the system.

1. **Install the microSDHC card.**
2. **Swipe down from the top of the Home screen, and tap the Settings (gear) icon.**
3. **Choose General and then Storage.**
4. **Slide the right panel up to reveal the options under SD Card.**
5. **Tap Mount SD Card.**

Unmounting and ejecting a microSDHC card

Removing a microSDHC card from a Galaxy Tab 4 NOOK without unmounting it might damage the information on your card, especially if you remove the memory while the system is powered on.

To unmount an SD card before it is physically removed from the tablet, do this:

1. **Swipe down from the top of the Home screen**
2. **Tap the Settings (gear) icon.**

3. **Choose General, then Storage.**

4. **Slide the right panel up to reveal the options under SD Card.**

5. **Tap Unmount SD Card. See Figure 1-10.**

6. **Select OK.**

7. **Open the slot and carefully push on the card to release it from the slot.**

    Place the card in the protective case it came in (or in a clean plastic bag) and put it away for future use. Close the small covering lid and snap it into place.

Figure 1-10: The Unmount option is in settings.

Formatting a microSDHC card

When you buy a new microSDHC, it will likely come *formatted* (a process that electronically indexes its memory so that the computer inside your tablet knows where to store or retrieve information). In that case, it's ready to use.

If you insert an unformatted microSDHC card, the Galaxy Tab 4 NOOK will alert you. No biggie. To format a microSD memory card when the system asks, follow these steps:

1. **Tap the Format Now icon.**

    You're asked if you are sure. Sure you're sure!

2. **Tap Format Now.**

If you want to completely wipe the contents of the card, manually format it. You might be clearing the card to give it to someone else, or perhaps installing a used card from another person. Or you might want to remove all traces of a top secret missile launch protocol sent to you as a gag by your daughter's teenage hacker boyfriend.

Here's how to start manual formatting:

1. **Swipe down from the top of the Home screen.**

2. **Tap the Settings (gear) icon.**

3. **Choose General, then Storage.**

4. **Slide the right panel up to reveal the options under SD Card.**

5. **Tap Format SD Card.**

    You're asked if you really want to do this. Stop and think whether you really do.

6. **Tap Format SD Card again.**

7. **Tap Delete All.**

Formatting a microSDHC card permanently deletes all data and any apps that are stored on it.

Yes, I'm aware that there are some service bureaus that *may* be able to recover data from a formatted or erased card, but I would hate to see you have to rely on their less-than-certain capability.

2

Laying Hands on the Screen

. . . .

In This Chapter

▶ Gesturing on your touchscreen

▶ Working with menus

▶ Opening more than one window

. . . .

Don't judge the capability of a device by the number of buttons you see. On the Samsung Galaxy Tab 4 NOOK, most of the action is in your hands. This chapter looks at touching the touchscreen. The next chapter covers tapping (and swiping and talking to) the keyboard.

 Like any piece of advanced electronics, your NOOK tablet's touchscreen could be damaged if it touches a high-voltage device. Don't leave it on top of a TV or a microwave oven, and don't play static electricity games with socks on a carpet.

Keying In on the Basics

Your tablet has two physical keys on its right side: Power/Lock and Volume. Three keys sit below the LCD screen. That's it. Picasso would be proud.

Table 2-1 lists their names and functions. The location I provide is based on holding the tablet in portrait mode (taller than wide) with the word Samsung at the top.

 If you're coming to the Samsung Galaxy Tab 4 NOOK from an earlier model of the Galaxy Tab or from an older Samsung Galaxy smartphone, the Menu key has been replaced by the Recent key on the front of the device below the LCD screen. Your Tab 4 NOOK will keep reminding you of this change until you finally put a check mark in the Do Not Show Again check box.

Table 2-1		Galaxy Tab 4 NOOK Keys	
Icon	*Name*	*Location*	*Actions*
n/a	Power/ Lock key	Top of the right side of tablet	Press and hold to turn tablet on.
			Press and hold to turn tablet off.
			Press and release to put the tablet to sleep.
			Press and release to wake the tablet from sleep.
n/a	Volume key	Right side of tablet, below Power/Lock key	Press + to increase volume.
			Press – to decrease volume.
⌐	Recent key	Left of center on front side of tablet, below screen	Display recently used apps.
			Open the Task Manager.
⬭	Home key	Center on front side of tablet, below screen	Go to the Home screen.
⬅	Back key	Right of center on front side of tablet, below screen	Return to the previous screen or option.

Gesturing at Your Touchscreen

About the glass on the Samsung Galaxy Tab 4 NOOK: It's pretty tough and not easy to scratch or break in ordinary usage, and if you drop your tablet onto a pile of bricks, it will probably scratch *and* break. Don't try to control it with a sharp object like a pen or a chisel or a pocket knife. Do touch its screen as you would anyone or anything about which you care dearly. Play nicely, in other words.

You have several (officially labeled) ways to communicate with a touchscreen, with slight variations depending on the particular app or control panel in use:

  ✓ **Scroll:** Touch a blank part of the screen — a place without an icon or command — and move your finger left or right. Some people slide gently and easily (their finger, that is), while others like to flick as if they were clearing a crumb from the table and onto the floor. (I'm not endorsing, just explaining.)

- **Touch:** To open an application, select an item from a menu, approve a command shown as an onscreen button, or to enter a character from the onscreen keyboard, touch or tap an object or icon on the screen.

- **Touch and hold:** Keep your finger on whatever you've touched to make a menu appear. Another use of a touch and hold is to select an item that can then be moved or dragged to another location. Another name for *touch and hold* is a *long press*.

- **Drag:** You can move an item, icon, *thumbnail* (tiny picture) or other element that you select with a touch and hold. Don't lift your finger from the screen before the item is comfortably in its new place.

- **Double-tap:** Touch an item on the screen twice in quick succession. A double-tap zooms in on an image; do it again to zoom back out.

- **Swipe:** Touch your finger on an item and drag it to another spot. Depending on the situation, you can swipe left or right, or up or down. Some apps might call this a *slide*.

- **Spread:** This is a two-finger maneuver. Touch the screen with two fingers and move them away from each other to zoom in on or enlarge an image.

- **Pinch:** Touch the screen with two fingers and move them toward each other to zoom out from or reduce an image (the opposite of a spread).

- **Rotate:** Place two fingers on the screen — perhaps your thumb and forefinger — and twist them as if you were turning a dial. If the app supports this gesture, the image will rotate on the screen.

- **Sweep:** Pass or sweep your whole hand across the whole screen, just lightly touching its surface. In some situations this captures a screenshot.

- **Cover:** Cover the screen with the palm of your hand to pause the playback of a video or music file.

A book is usually printed in portrait orientation (taller than wide) and a computer monitor is usually landscape (wider than tall). One of the beauties of a tablet is that you can often have it either way. Some applications — games and some video web pages like YouTube — are locked into one orientation or another, but others allow you to choose.

If you don't want the image on the screen to reorient itself, you can turn off screen rotation. Pull down the notification panel from the top of the screen and tap the screen rotation icon. When it's enabled, the icon is green; when it's disabled, it turns gray with ennui. To turn it back on, just go back to the panel and tap it again.

Starting at Home Base

Home, sweet home. Home base. Home-made rhubarb and cranberry pie. All kinds of great things begin at home, including the Samsung Galaxy Tab 4 NOOK.

The Home screen is the first thing you'll see after you turn on your tablet, and it's where you'll go when you close an app. It holds folders full of apps, is where one or more web browsers lives, and is the launching pad for the NOOK eReader (and other reading apps).

The main Home screen for the Galaxy Tab 4 NOOK is shown in Figure 2-1. Everyone's Home screen starts out looking the same, but you have an almost infinite number of ways to customize it.

Figure 2-1: The Home screen offers up apps.

The first thing I do on any tablet, smartphone, or computer is put my own *wallpaper* behind the home screen. I do this because it makes me feel at home. The wallpaper you see in Figure 2-1 is a stylized version of a photograph I took of a field of sunflowers near Seville, Spain. You can see a larger version at www.about.me/coreysandler.

You can add another, *secondary,* Home screen by pressing and holding on any Home screen. When the menu appears, choose Page. Scroll left or right to see more Home screens.

Wallpapering your Home screen

You can change the wallpaper for your Home screen several ways:

- On the Home screen, press and hold on any unoccupied section (not on an icon, for example). Assign a wallpaper for the Home screen, the Lock screen, or both. Then tell the system where the image is.

- On the Home screen, swipe down from the top to display the Settings (gear) icon. Tap the Device tab. In the left panel, tap Wallpaper and follow the instructions.

✔ Your Tab 4 NOOK comes with a set of abstract color wallpapers, and you can download free or paid wallpapers from the Play Store and the NOOK Shop. Any image viewable in the Gallery can be used as wallpaper.

Crawl space: Bottom of the Home screen

Let me take you on a tour of the parts of the Home screen, starting at the bottom and working your way up. You can refer back to Figure 2-1 for an illustration.

Look down at the very bottom of the screen: If you see a very small symbol of a *home,* then you have arrived at the official Home screen. If instead you see a horizontal bar, you're on a secondary Home screen.

✔ **NOOK Book icon:** Tap the icon to be nearly instantly transported to the most recently opened book, magazine, catalog, or other piece of reading material in your NOOK Library. It'll go to the last page you were reading before you did something else on your tablet.

The NOOK Book icon won't take you to a book you downloaded from Google's Play Store, or from your local library, or another source. This is for NOOK uses only.

✔ **Apps icon:** Tap the icon made up of 16 very small rectangles to see your apps. See Figure 2-2. You probably won't be able to see all the apps on one screen. Scroll or flick left or right to see more. As long as you're just lightly touching the screen, and not pointing with conviction at a particular icon, you can scroll easily.

Start any app by tapping its icon here (or tap its shortcut on the Home screen). Either method brings you to the same end: *appyness.*

Figure 2-2: I display my apps in alphabetical order; you can do otherwise if you choose.

While you're looking at your Apps screen, move your eyes almost all the way to the top of the screen: look just below the time in the upper-right corner. Here's what to look for here, from *right to left below the time* within the Apps screen:

✔ **Menu icon.** What you get when you tap the Menu icon depends on what page you're on. I've reordered the options in a more logical manner, which means what you see onscreen will be in a different order. Doesn't matter, really. My order is better.

• **View Type.** This one should have been first. If you choose a customizable grid, you can reorder the apps any way you want. Or, you can choose Alphabetical.

• **Edit.** You can create a folder and move some apps into it to neaten up the place; for example, you could put all of the Google apps in one folder and all of the NOOK apps in another. Any organizational scheme that makes sense to you is fine.

You can rearrange the order of apps to put the most important ones first or to put all reading apps next to each other — except that you can only rearrange apps if you have previously chosen Customizable Grid from the View Type option.

• **Create Folder.** Tap here to make and name a folder. See Figure 2-3. Press and hold icons, and drag them to the folder. You can put reading tools in one folder, web browsers in another. Or you can leave all of your apps scattered about, which is the way my desktop here in my office looks whenever I am in the middle of a big project. Whatever works for you.

• **Set Wallpaper.** Just for good measure, here's another way to set the wallpaper background for the Home screen, the Lock screen, or both.

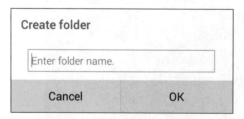

Figure 2-3: Tidy things up with folders.

✔ **Downloaded Items icon.** Maybe you want to see only those apps you've downloaded (not the ones that were already on the tablet when you got it). Sometimes an icon appears here that was actually brought to your device by Samsung, Google, or NOOK. Don't know why, and it doesn't matter.

Press the Back key to return to the display of apps. Move your eyes toward the center of the screen. You'll see a large tab called Widgets, and to the left of that a large tab called Apps. You can switch back and forth between these two by tapping one or the other tab name.

A *widget* is a tiny specialized delivery system for small bits of information. Your Tab 4 NOOK comes with widgets you can install on the Home screen — things like a thumbnail of your calendar, a dual clock display for globetrotters, weather and temperature reports, and the like.

One step up from the bottom: Shortcuts

Above the NOOK Book icon and the Home screen indicator is a row of (as many as six) icons for apps.

If you don't see the app you want to open, scroll left or right. If you don't see the app at all, you can add it to one of the Home screens. On the Apps screen, press and hold the icon you want; a *copy* of the icon appears on the Home screen.

Midscreen: A word from our sponsors

Above the apps shortcuts you'll see a message from the sponsor: Barnes & Noble sales or offers. This section changes. You can, if you want, tap an ad. You can also ignore the banner.

It's tough to completely delete the Barnes & Noble ads from your Home screen, but it's easy to move them to one of the secondary Home screens. That way they're there only when you want.

About two-thirds of the way up the main Home screen you'll see the covers of books, magazines, catalogs, videos, apps, and other things you have in your own NOOK Library. Here's what you can do with that:

- ✏ Tap the cover of any item to open it. If it's a book, the NOOK eReader opens. If it's a video, it will get ready to play. If the item has a small downward arrow in the corner of its image, it's waiting for you to download it.

- ✏ Tap the arrow at the end of the shelf to see other items in your collection.

- ✏ Tap the books icon at the right end of the shelf to open a more fulsome display of all of the titles in your library.

And, if you wish, you can remove the NOOK library from the Home screen. Press and hold it; then drag it to another screen or move it up to the trash can. See Figure 2-4. Removing the NOOK library from the Home screen *doesn't* remove NOOK capabilities from your tablet. You can still open NOOK apps individually or from the Apps menu.

Figure 2-4: The NOOK library has prime real estate on the main Home screen.

The Google search bar

The official search engine of the Samsung Galaxy Tab 4 NOOK is Google, but you can use a different search engine if you prefer.

Google Search only works if your tablet has an active Wi-Fi connection.

The main Home screen has a Google search bar near the top. It's pointed out in Figure 2-1. You'll recognize it because it says Google on the left, has space in the middle for a search term, and has a microphone icon on the right. See Figure 2-5.

Figure 2-5: The Google Search app accepts typing or dictation.

Dictation is a very convenient way to conduct a search.

1. **Tap your finger in the blank space on the Google bar.**

2. **Speaking clearly and directly at your tablet, say,** "Okay Google."

   If you do it right, you'll hear a beep and the microphone symbol turns red.

3. **Speak your search command.**

   Depending on whether you ask a question or state some search terms, and also depending on the speech recognition engine, you may get a spoken answer or a screen full of search results.

The notification bar and panel

At the tiptop leftmost part of the Home screen, you'll see notification icons. Have any new emails come in recently? Taken any screenshots? Has the system updated any apps for you? This is where to look. (In Figure 2-1, the notifications are from left to right: screenshot, email received, Gmail received.)

If you see a notification icon, you can delve deeper by pulling down the notification panel. Swipe down from the top of the screen with one finger (not two). Tap Email to go to the Email app, tap Screenshot to go to the Gallery and see the image, and so on. See Figure 2-6.

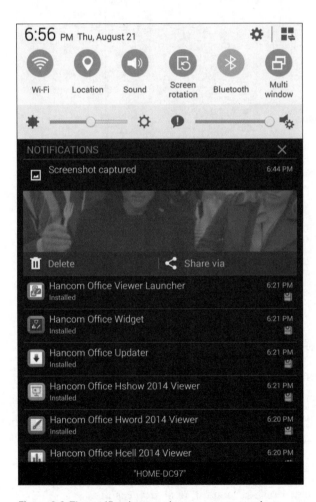

Figure 2-6: The notification panel recaps recent actions.

To clear away the notifications, tap the blue X in the upper-right corner of the notification panel. To temporarily put them out of the way, roll the panel back up to from where it came, or press the Back key; the notifications will still be there — and building up over time — but there's always tomorrow to deal with them.

Speaking of the notification panel, you can customize some of the apps or controls that appear there and adjust brightness of the screen and how loud the beeps, squawks, voices, and music are. Here's how:

1. **Swipe down from the top of the screen to display the notification panel.**

2. **Tap the Settings (gear) icon.**

3. **If it isn't already selected, tap the Devices tab at the top of the screen.**

4. **On the left panel, tap the notification panel.**

5. **Change the settings on the right side of the screen. See Figure 2-7.**

The status bar

As if owning a Samsung Galaxy Tab 4 NOOK weren't status enough, in the status bar you can see how well connected your tablet is, how full of energy it is, check its watch, and more.

The time of day

At the right corner of the status bar is the current time. You can customize that, too: Adjust the date and time, select a different time zone, use the 24-hour or military clock format, or change the date format.

1. **Swipe down from the top of the screen to show the notification panel.**

2. **Tap the Settings (gear) icon.**

3. **If it isn't already selected, tap the General tab at the top.**

4. **On the left panel, locate the Device Manager section and then tap Date and Time.**

5. **Change the settings on the right side of the screen.**

The life of a battery

I knew a guy in college, oh so many years ago, who seemed to live entirely on pork rinds. Your Tab 4 NOOK is much more sophisticated: It sups only on electrons.

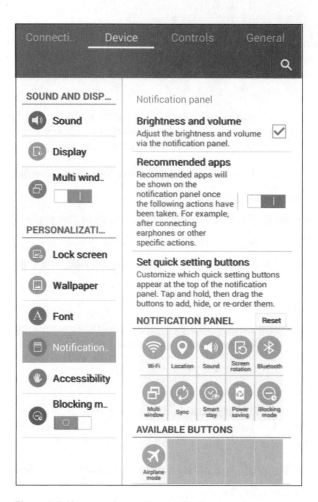

Figure 2-7: You can change the notification panel.

TIP

You can see how much power remains in the internal battery by looking at the can-shaped icon next to the time. If it's full, your tablet is full of power. If it's almost empty and looking a little red, recharge it. (If you're using the tablet while it's plugged into its recharger, you'll see a black lightning bolt within the battery icon, telling you that the juice is flowing in.)

WARNING!

Don't let the battery die back to nothingness. That can damage the battery. Also, don't try to replace the internal battery. It should last a few years. Contact Barnes & Noble or Samsung directly if the tablet needs a battery transplant.

Wi-Fi connection

Although you'll use the reading and other apps without an Internet connection, most of the time you'll want to be in communication by Wi-Fi. The icon's presence (a pie wedge with curved plates) means the Wi-Fi system is active and connected. If you see arrows moving up or down from the icon, that means information is exchanged with the Internet, including email services.

Depending on your settings, you may also see four other communication icons:

- **Wi-Fi Direct.** Similar to the standard Wi-Fi icon, this icon's arrows go left and right instead of up and down. This icon appears if you're using your tablet in local communication with another device that can exchange data without going on the Internet.

- **Bluetooth.** A stylized angular B tells you that the tablet's Bluetooth radio is active; you need to *pair* your tablet with another device and exchange security codes.

- **Connected to Computer.** A pitchfork-like symbol indicates that your Tab 4 NOOK is connected to a desktop or laptop computer. Confusingly, this icon can appear either in the notification panel (on the left) or the status bar (on the right), depending on the devices you're using.

- **Nearby Device.** If you've allowed nearby devices to come within the cone of connectivity of your Tab 4 NOOK via Wi-Fi, Wi-Fi Direct, or a mobile hotspot, you'll know it when you see this icon, a little tablet that seems to be doing the twist.

Other status or notification icons

Here are a few more you may see from time to time:

- **Mute Enabled.** A little speaker with a slash through its cone tells you audio has been silenced. (Wouldn't it be nice if you could aim that at the kids who want to loudly chat all through a red-eye flight to Istanbul?) You can mute your tablet by merely pressing and holding the – side of the Volume button until it is all the way off.

- **Alarm Activated.** Not a burglar alarm — a wake-up alarm. You can set an alarm, with a musical salute, from the Alarm Clock app. When it's on, a reminder appears on the notification panel.

- **Airplane Mode Activated.** If you turn on Airplane Mode (the quickest way is a two-finger pull from the top of the screen and then touching the icon) the tablet turns *off* Wi-Fi and Bluetooth radios but otherwise works. This way you can read books and use certain other apps, but block communication. A little jet airplane appears in the status bar to remind you that the radios are off. Retrace your finger-steps and turn *off* Airplane Mode to turn radios back *on*.

✔ **Blocking Mode.** Turn on this feature to block notifications, alarms, or both. Tap the Settings (gear) icon, choose the Device tab, and then tap Blocking Mode. Do this if you're in a place where noises are inappropriate, or if your tablet is on public display and you don't want other people to see your alarms or notifications. This icon, a slashed circle somewhat like a "Do not enter" sign, appears in the notification panel.

✔ **Error.** Houston, we have a problem. If you see a triangle with an exclamation point in it, do not panic. Yet. I've never seen one of these warnings on a Tab 4 NOOK, but if I did, here's what I'd do: Shut off the tablet, go for a brief walk around my office, and then turn it back on. Shutting off the device might clear memory of corrupted data. If the problem comes back, see the troubleshooting tips in Chapter 16 of this book; when all else fails, call Barnes & Noble or Samsung.

Grabbing a Quick Menu

You can pull down commands from the top of the screen with a one-finger salute: Swipe down to show the notification panel.

You can get to more on-off switches through here:

✔ Slide the panel of switches to the left.

✔ Touch the icon (three boxes and arrows) to the right of the Settings (gear) icon in the notification panel.

✔ From most screens, use a two-finger pull from the top. See Figure 2-8.

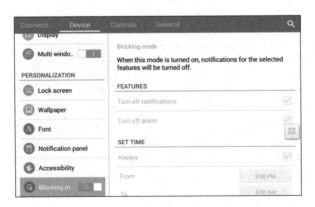

Figure 2-8: The quick panel offers controls for many functions that are available on most screens.

Flying the Tab 4 NOOK Wayback Machine

Mr. Peabody, the brainy beagle who took his owner, Mr. Sherman, on great adventures in the classic work of literature, "The Rocky and Bullwinkle Show" had his WABAC machine for time travel. That great device — one of the most advanced ever invented by a beagle — hasn't yet arrived on a Galaxy Tab 4 NOOK. The closest you have is the Recent key.

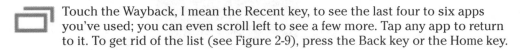 Touch the Wayback, I mean the Recent key, to see the last four to six apps you've used; you can even scroll left to see a few more. Tap any app to return to it. To get rid of the list (see Figure 2-9), press the Back key or the Home key.

Figure 2-9: The Recent key is at the bottom of the screen; press it to see apps you've used of late.

Opening Lots of Windows

How smart is the tiny processor inside your Tab 4 NOOK? It's *so smart* it can walk and chew gum at the same time. Or display a map of the fabulous island of Malta (it deserves a high spot on your bucket list) at the same time you research the price and availability of pickled white asparagus. I don't have the time or energy to explain how that particular combination of interests somehow managed to occupy my very crowded mind. But they did. And I used a special feature of Samsung tablets called *multi windows*. See Figure 2-10.

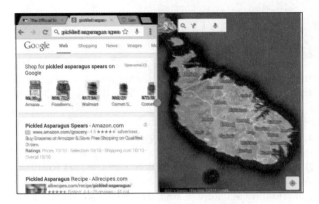

Figure 2-10: Of asparagus and the island of Malta, in a two-screen multi window.

You first have to turn on multi windows:

1. **Swipe down from the top of the screen to display the notification panel.**

2. **Tap the Settings (gear) icon.**

3. **If it isn't already selected, choose the Device tab at the top.**

4. **On the left panel, move the Multi Windows switch to the green On position.**

5. **Swipe in from the right side of any screen.**

   You see apps that you can run in multi windows. Tap the Menu icon at the bottom and then tap Edit to add or remove apps from the panel. See Figure 2-11.

Once it's on, you can turn the feature on or off by pulling down the notification panel from the top of the screen and tapping the Multi Windows icon. Green means it's available, gray means it's not.

Figure 2-11: The multi window launching pad slides in from the side of the screen. You change what apps appear there.

3

Typing by Tapping, Talking, Swiping

In This Chapter

▶ Moving, changing, and generally messing around with the keyboard

▶ Practicing penmanship

▶ Dictating instead of typing

*H*ow do you get your thoughts and wishes from your brain to your fingers and into the tablet? You've got a virtual, swipeable, handwritable, and voice-recognizable.

- ✔ *Virtual,* as in an onscreen keyboard that appears when needed; it usually pops up at the bottom of the screen where you need to enter text, but in most situations you can also float and move it.

- ✔ *Swipeable,* as in a feature that allows you to slide your finger from letter to letter.

- ✔ *Handwritable,* as in a touchpad that changes your writing — block letters or even most forms of cursive — into words.

- ✔ *Voice-recognizable,* as in the tablet listening to your voice and spitting out words.

Finding the Keyboard to the Kingdom

Figure 3-1 shows the Samsung keyboard, which is more of a traditional, typewriter-like keyboard.

Keep these tips in mind:

- ✔ How do you **hide the keyboard**? It depends. Try tapping the Enter/ Return or Done key. Press the Back (arrow) key at the bottom of the screen.

- To shift into **uppercase characters**, tap the up arrow at the left or right side of the keyboard. The first letter of the next word you tap will be in uppercase, and the next will be lowercase letters.

- To type in **all caps,** press and hold the up arrow on the keyboard. Tap one or the other arrow to turn off caps lock.

- To type an **accented character,** press and hold on a letter. Slide your finger onto the special character and release it when the one you want is highlighted. See Figure 3-2 for examples of accented characters in their lowercase and uppercase versions.

- To **insert a symbol,** tap the Sym key. In Figure 3-3 you can see some of the available symbol keyboards.

- To **insert an *emoji*** (also known as an *emoticon*), press and hold the Settings (gear) icon to the left of the spacebar. Tap the happy face to display emojis like those in Figure 3-4.

Tap for symbols   Settings icon   Tap for uppercase

Tap for uppercase

Figure 3-1: The basic keyboard of the Tab 4 NOOK, with lowercase and uppercase characters.

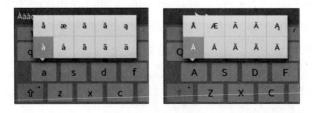

Figure 3-2: Accented lowercase *a* and uppercase *A* characters.

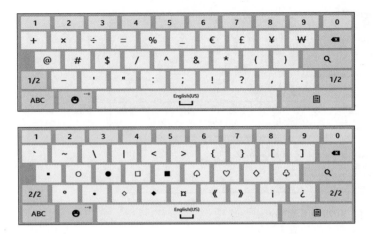

Figure 3-3: At the bottom left, you see 1/2 or 2/2, meaning the first or second of two screens.

Figure 3-4: These are formally known as *emojis*.

Adjusting the Keyboard

As a lifelong user of typewriters and then computer keyboards, I know the advantage of a well-designed physical board with well-spaced keys and a good solid clicky response. I can touch-type at a remarkable speed (and even hit the right keys most of the time.) That said, it is truly amazing to switch over to a virtual keyboard on a tablet and experience its ability to adapt.

The quickest route to keyboard settings is from the onscreen keyboard. Notice the Settings (gear) icon to the left of the large spacebar in Figure 3-1? Tap it to display the keyboard settings shown in Figure 3-5.

The following sections talk about the four main keyboard settings sections.

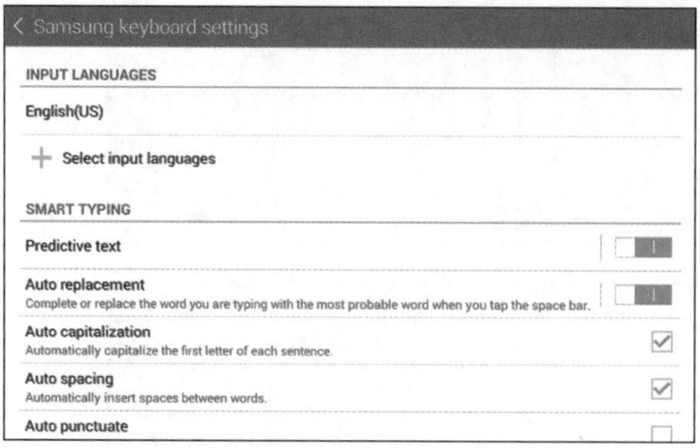

Figure 3-5: Keyboard settings.

Input Languages

Your Samsung Galaxy Tab 4 NOOK will most likely arrive with U.S. English as its default language.

✔ To **add other keyboards,** tap the Settings (gear) icon on the keyboard and then tap the green + mark.

✔ When you add a language, you're asked if you want to **update the list of available character sets.** Go ahead and do so; you might find some very interesting choices, including some languages you might never have heard of.

✔ **Choose a new keyboard** by touching and holding (a long press) the spacebar; then slide left or right.

✔ To **turn on or off a foreign language keyboard** that you've downloaded, tap the Settings (gear) icon on the keyboard; tap the + Select Input Languages command. Then add or remove a check-mark beside a language. In Figure 3-6, you see one at work.

Figure 3-6: It's all Greek to me. You knew I'd say that, right?

You must have at least one language selected. Be careful here; you could accidentally remove the check-mark from English if you have another language enabled. If you do that and find yourself unable to communicate, you'll have to retrace your steps to this screen to re-enable English.

Smart Typing

Think you're so smart? The onscreen keyboard, working with the microprocessor, can do things like this if you turn on those features:

- **Predictive text.** The tablet will try to guess what word you're typing as you type. Keep an eye on the black panel in the middle of the screen. If you see the word you want, tap the word.

  From time to time, you're certain to let a misspelled or just plain odd word slip through. Your tablet will think that is exactly what you meant to say. If you see a suggestion for a word that's wrong — one that you don't want to have to deal with again — press and hold your finger on that word. When the tablet offers to remove it, tap OK.

- **Auto replacement.** You type _Thank_ and the tablet guesses you next want to say _you._ If so, tap that word and proceed.

- **Auto capitalization.** Put a check in the box to automatically capitalize the first letter of any sentence.

- **Auto spacing.** This option is important when you use dictation or swiping (which you read about in this chapter). The tablet adds a space between each word without you having to press the spacebar.

- **Auto punctuate.** The tablet inserts a period (also known as a _full stop_) anytime you tap the spacebar twice.

Keyboard Swipe

There's no easy way around this: Some people absolutely swear by Samsung's Swipe keyboard, and other swear at it. Over the years, I've done both, but it's kind of growing on me. Even if it sometimes converts my pearls of wisdom into _portals of weirdness._

If you turn on _continuous input,_ you can draw words by moving your finger on the keyboard from letter to letter. To type _cat,_ you tap the letter _c_ and then proceed diagonally leftward to _a_ and then diagonally rightward to _t._ Lift your finger and if the universe is properly aligned, the word for a domesticated (or not) feline appears in whatever document you are working on. See Figure 3-7.

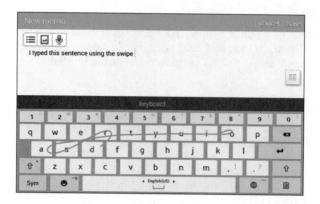

Figure 3-7: You can see my swiping path, where I was finishing up the word *keyboard.*

Practice for a while, and spend time telling the system to throw away errors and not keep throwing them back at you, and certainly not to get all huffy about it. I mean, who's in charge here anyway? Start slowly. Even then, you'll probably end up with more characters than you would using the old one-finger hunt-and-peck method.

Here are a few advanced tips:

- **Capital letters.** To go into uppercase, tap a letter and then drag your finger above the keyboard.

- **Double letters.** If you want to spell a word with double letters, make a little loop on the doubled character.

Key-Tap Feedback

Strictly a matter of personal preference, but you might want to hear a little click each time you press a key. The second option, in the Key-Tap Feedback section (under Settings) is Character Preview. When you tap a character, the letter or symbol is shown in a cartoon-like bubble.

Changing Keyboard Input

You can radically change the way your tablet receives your input. The following sections show you how to float a keyboard, how to speak instead of type, and how to use handwriting. You get to those options this way:

1. **Display the regular keyboard on screen.**

2. **Press and hold the Settings or Options button on the keyboard (left of the spacebar).**

   In Figure 3-8, you can see the standard selection.

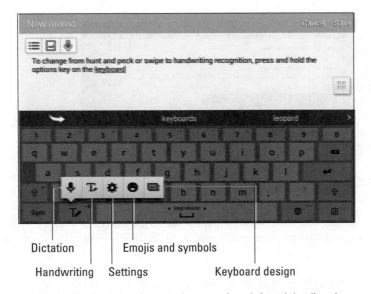

Dictation

Handwriting Settings

Emojis and symbols

Keyboard design

Figure 3-8: The keyboard input options are, from left to right: dictation, handwriting, settings, emoticons and symbols, and keyboard design.

Moving the keyboard

You can't shrink a keyboard with a pinch of your fingers, but you can make it *float*, which gives you a smaller, movable version. See Figure 3-9.

To produce a floater, do this:

1. **Display the regular keyboard.**

2. **Press and hold the Settings (gear) icon on the keyboard (left of the spacebar).**

   A menu appears.

3. **Tap the icon that shows a stack of keyboards.**

   That icon is ordinarily all the way to the right.

4. **Tap Floating.**

When the floating keyboard is onscreen, you can move it by pressing and holding the little tab at its top. To return to the regular keyboard, press and hold the Settings icon on the floating keyboard, tap the icon with the *tiny* stack of keyboards, and tap QWERTY.

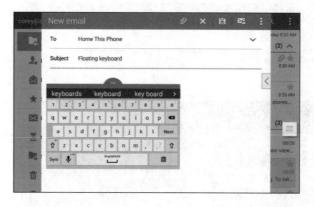

Figure 3-9: A floating keyboard may help when the full-size keyboard is taking up too much space or blocking your view.

Improving your penmanship

Now for something completely beyond the ability of the computer keyboard I am using to write these words. Your tablet's operating system can read words that you write.

Use your finger; never use a pen or stylus!

It's really cool, and it usually works. Here's how:

1. **Display the regular keyboard.**

2. **Press and hold the Settings (gear) icon on the keyboard (left of the spacebar).**

   A menu appears.

3. **Tap the icon that shows the letter T beside a tiny little pen.**

   The keyboard is replaced by an electronic version of a yellow legal pad.

4. **Touch your finger to the pad and start drawing characters. See Figure 3-10.**

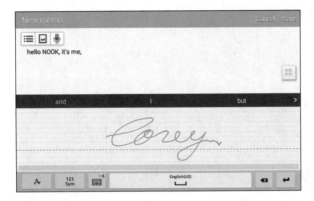

Figure 3-10: I used a combination of cursive and individual block characters.

These tips can help:

- ✓ You can either print individual characters, or use your best (or worst) form of cursive. If you use individual characters, you're going to need to practice a bit to avoid pausing too long between letters; a pause is considered to be the end of the word.

- ✓ If your chicken scratch gets misread, tap a suggested word in the panel, or tap the backspace key.

- ✓ The dashed line differentiates between uppercase and lowercase letters, or to enter punctuation. To spell my name, I could either make a significant difference in size between the C and the rest of the characters, or place the *C* above the line and the *orey* below it.

- ✓ A short hooked mark above the line is interpreted as a single or double quote. That same hook placed below the line is read as a comma.

Once the device has interpreted your handwriting, it displays a cleaned-up version with much better penmanship. See Figure 3-11.

Talking it out

I saved my favorite "typing" method for last: issuing verbal orders. This used to be the stuff of science fiction. "Open the pod bay doors, HAL."

A microphone icon appears only in apps that accept voice input. And the feature works best when your tablet has a Wi-Fi connection. Only certain apps allow basic dictation without a Wi-Fi connection.

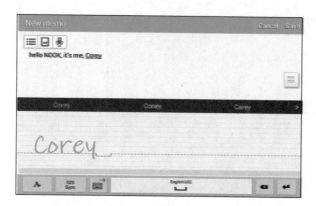

Figure 3-11: A sentence entered through the handwriting panel, including capital letters and punctuation.

Dictating

Here's how to dictate a sentence into a memo, an email, or most other apps that are set up to use the keyboard:

1. **Display the regular keyboard.**

2. **Press and hold the Settings (gear) icon on the keyboard (left of the spacebar).**

3. **Tap the microphone icon.**

   A larger red microphone appears, in anticipation of your words.

4. **Speak now.**

   Talk toward the microphone, which is the tiny hole just above the Power/Lock key on the side of the tablet.

Keep these tips in mind when you're talking to your Tab:

- **Be brief.** If you pause for a few seconds, the tablet will assume you've finished your sentence. If you speak too quickly or say too many words, the tablet may stop listening. See Figure 3-12.

- **Say your punctuation.** Pause briefly after a word before you say *comma* (or exclamation mark or question mark or semicolon or . . .).

- Touch in the upper panel to **edit words.** Press the Settings icon again if you want to open the keyboard for final touches.

- If you want to **use another language** for dictation, your Tab 4 NOOK is happy to give it a try. Tap the Settings icon and then tap Select Input Languages to add a new language.

Lately, I've been using the dictation feature on the Tab 4 NOOK to practice my accent in speaking French. I figure if the device can correctly decipher what I am saying, my pronunciation is close to the mark. C'est bon!

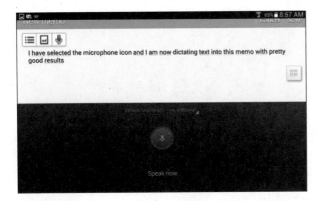

Figure 3-12: When the microphone glows red, your tablet is ready. I'll bet HAL would open the pod bay doors for me.

To censor or not

Watch your mouth! Google Voice has a setting that allows you to block offensive words. Strictly in the interest of research, I tried it out, and the da**ed thing wouldn't include all of my words. Or you can turn off the block command and curse to your heart's content. By the way, Apple and Amazon *aren't* considered offensive words, even on a device made by Samsung and sold by Barnes & Noble.

To turn the censor on or off (sounds dirty to me) here's what to do:

1. **Swipe down from the top of the screen to display the notification panel.**
2. **Tap the Settings (gear) icon.**
3. **If not already selected, choose the Controls tab at the top.**
4. **Tap the Language and Input section on the left side.**
5. **Make sure there is a check mark beside Google Voice Typing.**
6. **Tap the Settings (gear) icon beside that item.**
7. **In the Block Offensive Words section, add or remove the check mark for that item.**

   Back out of the settings screen by pressing the Home key or the Back key.

4

Getting Set to Go

I am not the first, nor will I be the last to point out that human beings have been able to read papyrus, chiseled inscriptions on stones, road signs, hand-illustrated, and then machine-printed books for tens of centuries without the need for batteries and an on-off button. Can we agree with the following? A NOOK tablet is not a book. (Hey, I just might have finally figured out what NOOK means: not a book.)

And because the tablet has so many advanced features, as a user your first interaction with the Tab 4 NOOK (and many later adjustments) involve *configuring* — setting up — the device so that it looks and acts the way you want.

Being a First Timer

Everybody has a first time, sooner or later. It's exciting and terrifying and often awkward. But it has to be done, and eventually (often sometime around the second time) it all becomes familiar because you have now learned what goes where, and when.

It's that way, too, with the Samsung Galaxy Tab 4 NOOK.

In this section, I discuss the steps you need to go through for the *very first time* you turn on your new tablet. The first time is different because it involves registering the device with at least three separate providers. You may want to add other accounts (like Facebook, Twitter, ad Dropbox). I suggest that you keep it simple, sweetheart. Add optional services later, once you have your NOOK tablet up and running.

Setting up a Google account

Your Google account includes access to Gmail, the photo service Picasa, Google Calendar, and uploading video to YouTube.

You can sign up for a Google account from your Samsung Galaxy Tab 4 NOOK, but it's easier to preregister from a regular computer. Regardless, it's a good idea to use the same username and password on both devices. If you also have a smartphone, use the same account. This allows you to synchronize calendars, Gmail, and apps you install on your tablet or phone, or both.

1. **Open a web browser and go to** www.google.com.

2. **Click the Sign In link.**

3. **Click the Create New Account link.**

4. **Choose a login name and password.**

    Now you can use that same account in registering your NOOK tablet.

The fact that you have so much information and perhaps one or more credit cards included in your Google account should tell you one important thing: Use a complex password and change it from time to time.

The first sign-on

Your tablet has been fully charged, right? If not, get thee to Chapter 1.

1. **Press and hold the Power/Lock key to turn on the tablet.**

    The key is on the thin right side of the tablet as you look at the screen.

    Brace yourself: It's going to take a while before the tablet comes to life for the very first time. Four, five, maybe even six or eight whole seconds. Think of it as a cute little puppy waking up from a dreamy sleep; it's going to take just a little bit of extra time while it figures out who it is, where it is, who you are, and if it feels all warm and fuzzy. When that is all done, it's going to roll over on its back and let you rub its tummy. The puppy, that is. Your Tab 4 NOOK is going to just sit there, but it will eventually be ready to welcome the strokes and taps of your fingers.

2. **Now give your device a name, like I've done in Figure 4-1.**

    Why bother? This is how you'll recognize your tablet when you attach it by USB cable to a PC or laptop, or when you use Bluetooth or Wi-Fi Direct or other technologies for wireless interaction. I explain more about these technologies in Part II of this book.

3. **Touch the screen about two-thirds of the way down from the top and swipe from left to right.**

    You can use any finger on either hand.

Figure 4-1: Allow me to introduce myself: This is your tablet's ID
in Wi-Fi, Bluetooth, and wired communication with other devices.

Later in this chapter, I show you how to require a more demanding key to
unlock your tablet. You *lock* your tablet to protect against unauthorized use:
You don't want just anybody to be able to read your email or notes, riffle
through the books you have purchased, and perhaps most frighteningly, to
use your accounts to buy books or airline tickets or entire airliners.

The very first set of options — Accessibility — is mostly aimed at users who
might have difficulty reading small print, certain colors, or performing particular actions. I put accessibility options at the end of this chapter, and you can
go there for guidance any time you need to.

Firing Up the Wi-Fi

Owning a tablet without regular or at least occasional access to the Internet is kind of like owning a broken pencil: pretty pointless.

Without Wi-Fi, you can't register your device with Samsung for updates and apps and offers, sign in to B&N for NOOK Shop access, or contact Google and get stuff from them. You can't go to the Internet or get email without establishing a Wi-Fi link.

Four links in the Wi-Fi chain

When you first turn on your Tab 4 NOOK, you're guided right into the Wi-Fi setup.

Very important point here, please: You need four elements to successfully connect your Tab 4 NOOK to the Internet through a Wi-Fi system. You have to set them up correctly. This chapter helps you do that.

- ✔ **Turn on Wi-Fi on your tablet.** The Wi-Fi radio and software on your Tab 4 NOOK have to be turned on.

- ✔ **Be near a router.** You must be within range of a functioning Wi-Fi *router* (a signal transmitter/receiver).

- ✔ **Choose a signal.** You must connect to an available signal. Some Wi-Fi signals may be open to any user. Others (most, these days) require a password and sometimes a username or other details.

- ✔ **Use a working router.** The Wi-Fi router itself has to communicate with the Internet. Your tablet may connect to a router, but get no further than the box on the wall. If you can establish a link with a Wi-Fi system but get no further, check with the owner or operator of the router, or find another one to use.

The initial Samsung Galaxy Tab 4 NOOK is a Wi-Fi device; it doesn't have a cellular radio. I discuss Wi-Fi and the close-proximity Bluetooth in detail in Chapter 5 of this book. If you have a non-standard setup in your home, office, or elsewhere, you might want to go there now and return to this page later.

For 98.2 percent of users (I just made that number up, but by 98.2 I mean "nearly everyone") the process of connecting to a Wi-Fi system is quite simple. You probably already have one in your home or office. You'll also find them in most public libraries, many other public places, and in many stores and restaurants. Barnes & Noble, as part of its intense desire to get you to buy a NOOK tablet and visit their stores, offers free Wi-Fi access. You can even read free samples or certain books in their entirety while you're in the store.

Hunting for Wi-Fi

The steps you go through are very similar to what you have to do any time you use your tablet somewhere new. And so, I explain the process of finding and signing on to Wi-Fi. When you turn on your Galaxy Tab 4 NOOK, it hunts around for any available Wi-Fi networks. You will likely find three types:

- **Open networks** aren't protected by any password or login requirements. Just choose the network and you're on the Internet. It's *probably* safe, but be very careful about the sites you might visit; I would advise *not* doing your banking or making a purchase involving a credit card on an open network. If you have no choice, go ahead. Then plan on changing passwords and monitoring your credit card and bank statements regularly, which is something you should be doing anyhow.

- **Open networks with login** don't need a password, but the browser asks you to log in. You may have to provide your name, address, email address, and other information. In some cases, you may be asked to prove you are who you say you are by providing a smartphone number and then verifying that information by responding to a text message sent to the phone. Use your judgment about how much information you want to provide, and *don't assume this sort of system is protected from hackers.*

- **Locked networks** require a password, and sometimes other information such as a login name and security settings. If the locked network is in your own home or office, it's probably safe for things like banking and shopping.

  But still: Change your passwords and regularly monitor your credit card and banking statements.

Enabling Wi-Fi on the tablet

When you first sign on to your tablet, turn on the Wi-Fi circuitry.

Why does the Tab 4 NOOK have an on/off setting for this essential function? Because you might choose to save some battery power by turning it off. You can also turn off Wi-Fi by switching to Airplane Mode.

Here's how to set up your tablet to communicate with Wi-Fi:

1. **Swipe down from the top of the screen to display the notification panel.**

2. **Tap the Settings (gear) icon.**

3. **If it isn't already, choose the Connections tab at upper left.**

  4. **On the left panel, find the Wi-Fi slider switch.**

  5. **If it's grayed out, slide it to the right.**

  It usually takes a few seconds for the device to set up the system.

  On the right side of the screen, a panel shows all Wi-Fi networks within usable range. They might have clever or manufacturer names. See Figure 4-2. The strongest signal is first; the icon shows the signal strength. A small lock icon means the network is locked; you'll see the word Secured below the network name. You can tap the name to read details.

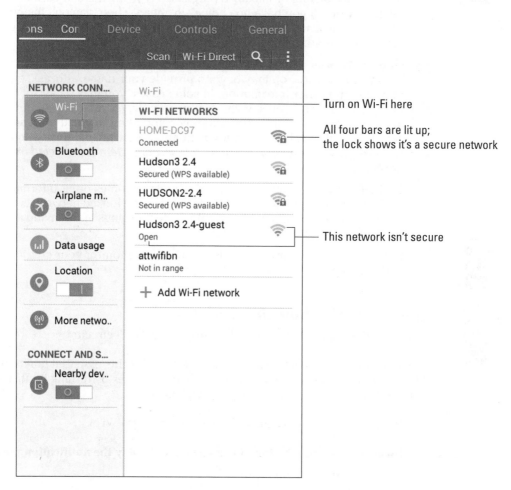

Figure 4-2: You'll see system names, signal strength, and whether the network needs a password.

6. **Tap the network you want to connect with.**

   If you do it right, the name of the network changes from black to a color, and you'll see Connected below its name.

   In most secured cases, all you need is the password. Some devices require additional settings. Tap Advanced to show more options, including Proxy and IP Settings.

If you return to a place where you've connected via Wi-Fi, your tablet will try to reconnect. And your tablet comes with details for a Wi-Fi hotspot called attwifibn, which is the free hotspot in nearly all Barnes & Noble bookstores.

Adding a Wi-Fi network manually

You can manually add a Wi-Fi network to your system. You have to know the name of the system (referred to in technobabble as *Network SSID*). Your type of security protocol and password that may be required. To add a system this way, tap the + Add Wi-Fi Network command (at the bottom of the list of detected networks). Tap Connect. See Figure 4-3.

Switching Wi-Fi systems

Once you're using a particular system, the tablet stays with it as long as it has a usable signal. If you notice the speed dropping, or if you get an onscreen message about a weak or unstable signal, go back to the Wi-Fi connections page and see if there's a stronger signal listed.

Reconnecting to a Wi-Fi system after setup

To turn on Wi-Fi, do this:

1. **Swipe down from the top of the screen to display the notification panel.**

   Or, swipe down with two fingers from the top of the screen to display the Quick menu.

2. **If the Wi-Fi icon isn't in color, tap it.**

If Airplane Mode is on, that icon is shown in color, but the Wi-Fi icon will be gray. You can turn on Wi-Fi within Airplane Mode, which kind of defeats the purpose of that option, by tapping the Wi-Fi icon.

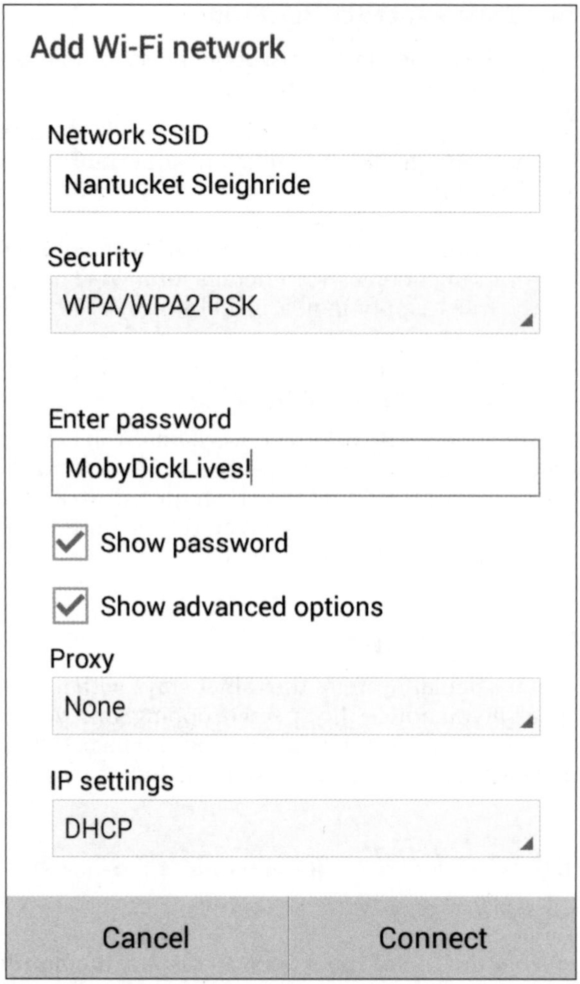

Add Wi-Fi network

Network SSID

Nantucket Sleighride

Security

WPA/WPA2 PSK

Enter password

MobyDickLives!

☑ Show password

☑ Show advanced options

Proxy

None

IP settings

DHCP

| Cancel | Connect |

Figure 4-3: When you manually enter a Wi-Fi network, enter its name (and maybe a password and advanced options).

Signing Up for Accounts and Other Preliminaries

Your tablet (or, actually, your tablet's owner) needs to agree to all sorts of legal fine print from hardware and software providers; sorry to have to tell you, but these agreements serve almost exclusively to protect *them* from claims by *us* for failure to satisfy. What a world!

And you need to set the internal clock and calendar and a few other house-keeping details.

Click here; read the fine print later

There's no way to avoid it: The lawyers will make you agree to their terms in the euphoniously named EULA (end-user license agreement). It's either that or put the tablet back in its box and try to convince Barnes & Noble or another seller to take it back.

There's nothing out of the ordinary in the terms, other than turning over the key to your house and the technical specs for the gravity-free hovercraft you've just designed. It's all in there, except for the part about the house and the hovercraft.

It's a take-it-or-leave it deal from Samsung, and later from Google and at the end of the line from Barnes & Noble for the NOOK Shop. Tap Confirm to agree.

Samsung offers some free apps to registered owners, and this is also a good way to assure that your tablet is automatically updated.

Use a credit card with premium insurance or buyer's assistance programs. For example, certain American Express, Visa, or MasterCards let you return purchases for a full refund, even if the store says otherwise. And some cards extend (usually by a year) the standard warranty of many products. Here's an instance where it does pay to read the fine print in an agreement, or call customer service of your card issuer to discuss these sorts of protections.

It's a Google world after all

If you already have a Google account, it generally makes sense to use that login and password across most or all of your digital devices. You can set up an account on the Tab 4 NOOK or perform the registration on a PC or laptop and then enter the name and password on your tablet.

When you first sign in to your tablet, you're offered the opportunity to create or sign in to an existing Google account. It's worthwhile, with two caveats:

- ✔ Think twice about revealing too much personal information to the public.
- ✔ Protect what you unveil with a strong password.

With a Google account you'll also be able to back up your data, including apps, app settings, system settings, and Wi-Fi passwords.

Another part of the Google registration asks if you want to allow apps to better determine your location. This is a good thing when you want to use an online map. The less-than-good thing is that Google or advertisers might want to place ads on pages that are frighteningly specific to your location. (In theory, the advertisers don't know your name or physical address, but it's still a bit somewhere between curious and unsettling to some.)

Signing up for a NOOK account

You did buy this particular model of the Samsung Galaxy Tab 4 because of its integration of the NOOK Shop, right? You're going to want to create a Barnes & Noble account.

If you already have an account, your tablet can retrieve any eBooks and periodicals already in your account from other NOOK devices or from PCs, laptops, or other tablets running a NOOK app.

You can create a B&N account from your personal computer ahead of time. Then all you need is your username and password when you set up your tablet. You can create a B&N account from www.bn.com, www.barnesandnoble. com, or www.nook.com. They all go to the same place.

1. **If you don't have a NOOK account, tap No, I Need to Create an Account.**

2. **Tap Create an Account.**

3. **Fill in the form with your name, email, a password, and other information.**

4. **Tap Submit. See Figure 4-4.**

In addition to the eReader on the Samsung Galaxy Tab 4 NOOK (and previous NOOK models), Barnes & Noble offers free software that lets you read (and buy) publications on devices including desktop and laptop PCs, Macintoshes, iPads, iPhones, and various Android devices. It's easy to start reading on one device and finish on another; what you can't do is have the same book or publication on two devices at the same time.

Who knows where the time goes?

Check the time that's displayed while you're setting up. Use the up or down arrows to adjust the time; pay attention to the AM or PM settings and tap that indicator if you need to change it.

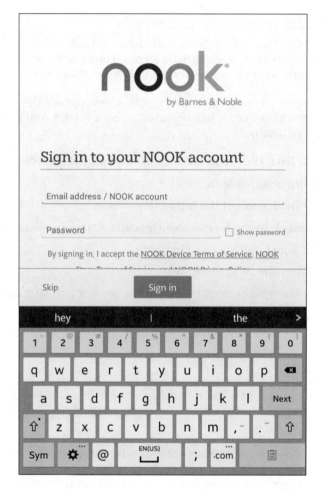

Figure 4-4: You'll use the onscreen keyboard to sign up for a new NOOK account if needed. Oh, and you'll need to agree to Barnes & Noble's terms of services.

Locking Things Down

Please allow me to ask a few questions:

- Will you ever loan your Tab 4 NOOK to someone else?
- Will anyone (family, friends, acquaintances, or perfect strangers) ever have access to your tablet when you're not around?
- Can you imagine that your tablet might someday (perish the thought) be lost or stolen?

Preparing the tablet for lockdown

The Galaxy Tab 4 NOOK, as delivered, uses the very basic one-finger left-to-right unlock pattern, which is essentially an open door. Anyone picking up your tablet is almost certain to quickly stumble upon that insecure gesture.

Unless you change the setting, your tablet will ordinarily lock the screen after the screen times out because it has detected no recent taps. You can adjust the interval before time out:

1. **Swipe down from the top of the screen to display the notification panel.**
2. **Tap the Settings (gear) icon.**
3. **Choose the Device tab at the top of the screen.**
4. **In the left panel, in the Sound and Display section, tap Display.**
5. **In the right panel, tap Screen Timeout.**
6. **Touch to fill in one of the bubbles.**

For most users, a safe amount of time is between 2 and 10 minutes.

You can manually lock the screen by briefly pressing the Power/Lock key on the right side of the tablet.

Changing the lock

Once you've set up your new Tab 4 NOOK, and before you leave it unguarded (or take it out of your home or office), I strongly suggest requiring a password.

To choose the unlock or security scheme for your tablet, do this:

1. **Swipe down from the top of the screen to display the notification panel.**
2. **Tap the Settings (gear) icon.**
3. **Choose the Device tab at the top of the screen.**
4. **In the left panel, in the Personalization section, tap Lock Screen.**
5. **In the right panel, in the Screen Security section, tap Screen Lock.**

You have lots of options for the screen lock and unlock:

- ✔ **Swipe.** This is no lock at all. You're improving upon this right now.

- ✔ **Pattern.** The screen displays nine dots in a three-by-three pattern. Set a pattern by tapping any one dot; keep your finger on the screen as you move to other dots on the screen. Don't use an obvious pattern like a box or a line. The pattern lock can start at any dot. See Figure 4-5.

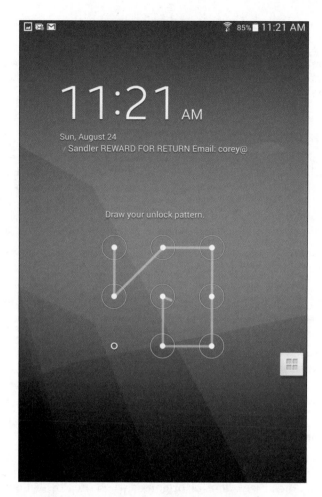

Figure 4-5: If you choose to use a pattern for unlocking your tablet, you can start at any of the nine dots and finish wherever you'd like to go; try something not very obvious.

✔ **PIN.** If you're numerically inclined, choose a personal identification number; you can use any combination of numbers with as many as 16 digits.

✔ **Password.** Create a password of as many as 16 characters, numbers, or symbols. Again, don't be obvious. "Password" isn't a good password. Neither is your name.

My favorite type of password is a phone number or address that has no direct connection to you but which you can recall from memory. An old phone number of a distant relative? The street address of the post office in the town you lived in three jobs ago? Oh, and don't write it down on a sticky note applied to the bottom of the tablet.

✔ **None.** This is really, truly no lock at all. Any time the tablet is turned on, anyone can use it. This may seem like a good choice to someone for some reason — not to me, though.

Customizing your unlock scheme

While you're choosing a pattern, password, or PIN unlocking scheme, you're offered other ways to customize how your tablet greets you. Here are the options:

✔ **Clock Widget.** You can choose a clock size for your Home screens, and decide whether you want to see the current date.

✔ **Personal Message.** You can put in, "Greetings, earthlings. I come in peace." Or anything else. Keep it clean, people.

✔ **Owner Information.** You can list your name and other information on the Lock screen, in hopes that a good Samaritan would return it. Tap Owner Information; then tap Show Owner Info on Lock Screen to enable or disable the option. Touch in the text field to type.

My owner information message has my name, email address, and *REWARD FOR RETURN*. I've never had to test whether the promise of a reward will entice someone to return my tablet, because I'm a pretty careful guy. I figure it can't hurt.

✔ **Lock Automatically.** Say how quickly to lock the screen after the screen automatically turns off.

✔ **Lock Instantly with Power/Lock Key.** Use this option to enable the Lock screen when the Power/Lock key is pressed. If you don't enable this option, the screen dims or brightens when the Power/Lock key is briefly pressed, but won't lock.

Depending on which lockdown method you select, you'll see one of these options:

✔ **Make Pattern Visible.** If you choose the pattern, this option lets you see the traces of your pattern as you draw it.

✔ **Make Passwords Visible.** If you choose to use the password, this option lets you see the characters as you type; they appear onscreen briefly and then disappear.

✔ **Make PIN Visible.** If you choose the PIN, this option lets you see the numbers as you enter them; they appear onscreen briefly and then disappear.

Encrypting Your Data

Making someone enter a pattern, PIN, or password before they can use your tablet is like locking the front door. But if you really want to secure your tablet's contents, consider encrypting the device, or the external microSDHC card, or both.

Why would you want to do this? If you are merely storing books to read and a few photographs, videos, and music files, this might be a bit of overkill. But if you plan to store personal or business files that would be damaging or embarrassing if seen without your permission, you can encrypt them. Now, it must be said that the level of encryption within an Android device isn't government spy-agency level. (And, as you know, even Top Secret government files can leak like a sieve.)

An encrypted Tab 4 NOOK, though, is difficult (if not impossible) for an amateur to read. Your strongest defense is a complex, unobvious password.

You can encrypt accounts, settings, downloaded applications (along with associated data), media, and other files. You can also encrypt the data stored on an external microSDHC card.

Encryption can take as much as an hour the first time you do it. Before you start, make sure your Samsung Galaxy Tab 4 NOOK is fully charged and leave it plugged into the wall adapter while the process is going on. If the encryption process is interrupted, you could lose some or all of your data.

Encrypting

Here's how to encrypt your tablet:

1. **Swipe down from the top of the screen to display the notification panel.**

2. **Tap the Settings (gear) icon.**

3. **Choose the General tab at the top of the screen.**

4. **In the left panel, in the Device Manager section, tap Security.**

5. **In the right panel, in the Encryption section, tap Encrypt Device or Encrypt External SD Card.**

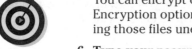

   You can encrypt only the data that's internal by checking the Fast Encryption option. You can also encrypt audio and video files, but leaving those files unencrypted speeds up the process.

6. **Type your password once.**

   The encryption password must be at least 6 characters and have at least 1 number. You're asked to enter it a second time.

Use a strong or complex password for encryption, and don't forget it. Don't use anything obvious, like your name or your pet's name or "Password." The best type of password is something that combines letters and numbers and isn't directly associated with you. And don't write the password on a sticky note on the back of your tablet.

7. **Type it again.**

   When the encryption process begins, your tablet will restart several times as it goes through various steps. You can't use the tablet while it's encrypting the device or the memory card.

Decrypting

If you later decide that you don't want encryption, you can reverse the process. You'll need the correct password, of course.

Here's how to undo the scrambling:

1. **Swipe down from the top of the screen to display the notification panel.**

2. **Tap the Settings (gear) icon.**

3. **Choose the General tab at the top of the screen.**

4. **In the left panel, in the Device Manager section, tap Security.**

5. **In the right panel, in the Encryption section, tap Decrypt Device or Decrypt External SD Card.**

   The decryption options only appear if you've encrypted the data. Follow the instructions that appear onscreen to remove the encryption.

Oh, and guess what? If it took your Tab 4 NOOK an hour or so to encrypt files, settings, and other items, it takes about the same amount of time to decrypt them. Make sure the tablet's battery is fully charged, and plug it into the wall power adapter.

Doing First Things Last: Accessibility Options

If you have impaired vision or need specific accommodations when using the touchscreen and other Tab 4 NOOK features, you have options. You'll have a chance to make these settings the very first time you turn on your Samsung Galaxy Tab 4 NOOK, but you can also make those changes later.

Here's how to get to the accessibility settings:

1. **Swipe down from the top of the screen and tap the Settings (gear) icon.**

2. **Choose the Device tab at the top of the screen.**

3. **On the left panel, tap Accessibility.**

4. **Choose an option from the sections in the right panel: Accessibility, Services, Vision, Hearing, Dexterity, or Recognition sections.**

The following sections explain customization features.

Accessibility

The first screen deals with some very basic settings:

- **Auto Rotate Screen.** This option is available in other places, too. Tap a check mark to rotate the view onscreen if you change the way you hold the tablet. If you don't want it to rotate, leave this option off.

- **Screen Timeout.** Select the period of time before the screen shuts off. I recommend at least two minutes, or perhaps more. It depends on how often you let your mind wander; I regularly drift off into very important but soon forgotten daydreams of several minutes in length.

- **Speak Passwords.** This setting seems misplaced; if you put a check mark in the box, and if you turn on Explore by Touch (which is an option you can find under other settings), the tablet will read out any entry you make in a password box.

- **Single Tap Mode.** This option lets a single tap stop or *snooze* (temporarily delay) an alarm or calendar reminder.

- **Show Shortcut.** This option adds accessibility options to the Power/ Lock key. If you *do* turn on advanced features like Explore by Touch, I recommend adding this shortcut to allow for a quick exit from that feature.

- **Manage Accessibility.** You can save all the changes you've made to vision, touch, and sound options and update the file as needed; you can also share your setup with another device if this file is created.

Services

There's only one Accessibility service in the Services section in the version of Android used in the initial release of the Tab 4 NOOK. More may come later.

When you turn on TalkBack, your tablet starts narrating virtually everything that's displayed on screen. It also confirms the names of icons you tap or actions you take. To turn on this feature, touch the switch at the top of the screen; an advisory will ask for permission to monitor your actions, inspect the contents of windows you're interacting with, and most importantly of all, turn on the Explore by Touch feature.

TalkBack and the associated Explore by Touch are truly impressive features of Android that are of great help to people who are visually impaired. If that's not you, I'll tell you that this is almost certainly *not* something you will want to turn on. Your tablet's behavior will be radically changed and its reactions will be (purposely) much slower.

If you want to explore TalkBack and Explore by Touch, I recommend first turning on Show Shortcut in the Accessibility section. This lets you change or reset your settings much more easily by pressing the Power/Lock key.

Vision

These options can enlarge text, reverse the colors to increase contrast, and let you adjust for color blindness. Here are the options:

- **Font Size.** The default setting is Small, but you can go up four stages to Huge or down two increments to Tiny.

- **Magnification Gestures.** Touch and slide the switch at the top of the panel to enable this feature. It lets you zoom in and out on an image by triple-tapping the screen; while zoomed in you can pan from side to side by dragging two or more fingers across the screen, and you can temporarily magnify something on the screen by triple-tapping and holding.

    Triple-tap doesn't enlarge the keyboard. Also, magnification gestures may slow down some apps.

- **Negative Colors.** Touch this option to change black to white, and change colors to versions some people may find easier to see. You can also manually change some colors in the next option.

- **Color Adjustment.** Tap to display a description of the available adjustments, and then move the slider switch to On if you want to proceed. You'll see color samples. It's recommended that people using this tool make adjustments in an environment with normal indoor lighting. See Figure 4-6.

- **Notification Reminder.** Move the slide switch to On to have the tablet beep — at an interval you select — to remind you of any unread notifications.

- **Text-to-Speech Options.** You can choose between the Samsung or Google text-to-speech engine. They both are quite capable; touch Listen to an example to select the one that's clearer to you. You can also adjust the Speech rate, the speed at which the computer voice jabbers.

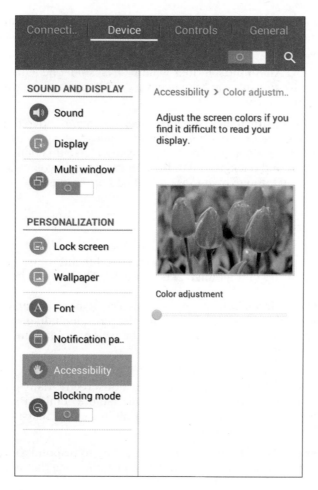

Figure 4-6: Color adjustment helps users compensate for certain types of visual impairments.

Hearing

The customization features here include adjustments for stereo and balance and the ability to turn on subtitles for apps that can. Here are the choices:

✓ **Sound Balance.** If you've got a set of earphones attached or are using an external set of speakers to play back music or the audio of a movie or television, you can adjust the sound balance; touch and hold the indicator and slide it left or right as desired. Touch Set to accept a change. Tap Cancel to back out and shut off the racket.

✓ **Mono Audio.** If you're listening to your tablet using a headset with only one earphone, you can merge the stereo channels into a single mono signal.

✓ **Turn Off All Sounds.** It does what it says; someone who is deaf or who otherwise doesn't want unnecessary noise can choose this option to mute the tablet.

✓ **Google Subtitles/Samsung Subtitles.** Touch and move the slide switch to enable one or the other or both schemes to display onscreen subtitles for certain apps. The Google system lets you change text size and the color and background of the subtitle; Samsung goes a few steps further by letting you choose a font and other effects.

Dexterity

Some of the settings here are quite helpful for users with physical infirmities that may limit the use of one hand or make it difficult to use the physical keys on the side or top of the tablet. See Figure 4-7. The choices here include:

✓ **Assistant Menu.** You can add a small Quick menu on most screens with larger, easier-to-use icons for many features, including volume control, power off, settings, and zoom. You can choose a dominant hand. It comes preset for righties.

If you turn on the accessibility Quick menu, you get an onscreen button for *screen capture* (a picture of what's onscreen). Many users find this single onscreen button easier to use than the combination of Power/Lock and Home; that combination requires more than a bit of dexterity and very precise timing.

✓ **Press and Hold Delay.** The tablet is set up to respond to a press-and-hold for certain functions; you can define just how long that hold has to be.

Interaction Control

This section lets you fine-tune some of the ways you use your hands on the tablet, including blocking areas of the screen so that they don't respond to touch; this is useful if you hold the tablet with one or more fingers on the screen at all times.

Turn on this feature by moving the slide switch at the top of the panel. Once it's on, you can turn the function on or off, or change the settings by pressing and holding the Home key and the Volume - key at the same time.

Note that you can't turn on the Assistant menu if interaction control is turned on; you'll be offered the chance to turn off the Assistant menu.

The Assistant menu gives you these buttons

Figure 4-7: Turning on the Assistant menu gives you a set of 12 large onscreen soft keys that many users may find easier to use than the physical keys on the front and side of the tablet.

Part II
Communicating Across the Galaxy

Handle email server connection trouble with Samsung recommendations at www.dummies.com/extras/samnsunggalaxytab4nook.

In this part . . .

- ✔ Connect with Wi-Fi and Bluetooth.
- ✔ Use the USB cable to connect your tablet to a computer.
- ✔ Add and change contacts.
- ✔ Browse the web and choose between mobile and standard sites.

5

Making Further Connections

*I*n addition to Wi-Fi from your Tab 4 NOOK to the Internet, your handheld wonder can use Wi-Fi Direct to communicate with many other devices in the immediate vicinity. The same handheld wonder can use a different kind of short-range radio system, called Bluetooth, to talk to and otherwise enjoy relations with more electronic thingies.

But as a reminder: the Samsung Galaxy Tab 4 NOOK *doesn't* have a cellular radio. Your smartphone does, and certain other more expensive tablets do, but not this NOOK.

This chapter expands your use of wireless non-cellular communication and then gets you *wired*.

Working without a Wire

Chapter 4 explains how to reach the Internet through a Wi-Fi wireless connection. I put that information there because everything else that follows is dependent upon at least that initial wireless setup.

Here, I discuss Wi-Fi generalities and then look at other options to connect your Tab 4 NOOK.

You can also usually find a Wi-Fi signal at public libraries, some government buildings and public spaces, and at many cafés. And Barnes & Noble, the seller of your Tab 4 NOOK, maintains a free Wi-Fi signal in nearly all of its stores.

If you need help creating a Wi-Fi network, call your Internet provider or call or visit Barnes & Noble, which promises to provide at least basic levels of support to all buyers of their NOOK devices.

Bottom line: use the signal that works best with your Tab 4 NOOK. The Wi-Fi app will seek out the strongest connection it can find, and usually switch if you move your tablet or other conditions change.

Advanced Wi-Fi settings

The Wi-Fi system should function well as delivered, but there are some advanced settings you can use to adjust performance to meet your needs. See Figure 5-1.

Figure 5-1: The Advanced settings for Wi-Fi allow you to keep your radio active, put it on a timer, and control scanning and connection options.

To reach the somewhat hidden screen, do this:

1. **Swipe down from the top to display the notifications panel.**

2. **Tap the Settings (gear) icon.**

3. **If it isn't already selected, choose the Connections tab at the top of the screen.**

4. **If it isn't already on, slide the Wi-Fi switch to the right.**

5. **Tap the Menu icon in the upper-right corner.**

6. **Select Advanced.**

7. **Choose your options:**

   - **Network Notification.** This brings up a message anytime an open network is detected within range.

   - **Sort By.** You can sort by signal strength or by the name of the router. In general, I care much more about the quality of the connection (its signal strength) than I do its name.

   - **Keep Wi-Fi on During Sleep.** Choose among Always (you get email and notifications while the tablet's asleep, which is a good thing except that it uses battery power); Only When Plugged In (which deals with the battery power issue, assuming an AC outlet is handy), or Never (which shuts off the radio and saves battery power).

   - **Always Allow Scanning.** If you put a check mark in this box, your tablet lets Google Location Services and other applications scan for Wi-Fi networks even when other radio features are off. This may allow certain mapping programs to keep track of where you are even without a Wi-Fi signal, although full maps features aren't available without an Internet connection.

   - **Wi-Fi Timer.** You can have your tablet turn on (and off) the Wi-Fi radio at a specified time. One possible use: to allow your device to check for email in the middle of the night but otherwise stay in Sleep mode, sipping slowly from the battery.

Wi-Fi Direct

Back in the early 1980s, when I was the first executive editor of *PC Magazine* (wow, that must mean I am *ancient*), it was common for the latest, greatest new hardware to be way out front of the software needed to use its features. Or to put it another way, we had many many solutions that were in search of a problem. So it is with some of the technologies now arriving in advanced portable devices including the Tab 4 NOOK.

Wi-Fi Direct lets your tablet connect directly to each other *without going through the router.* For example, your tablet could connect to your smartphone and use its facilities. Or your smartphone could pick up files from your tablet. And perhaps most intriguingly, you could send a file across the room to a Wi-Fi–enabled printer to produce a hard copy.)

Only one of the Wi-Fi devices has to be specifically designed for Wi-Fi Direct; the other needs plain old Wi-Fi capability.

As this book goes to press, the following is true: Your Samsung Galaxy Tab 4 NOOK has Wi-Fi Direct functions, but try as I might, I couldn't get the tablet to communicate directly with another device (including a current model Samsung smartphone) using this technology. See Figure 5-2.

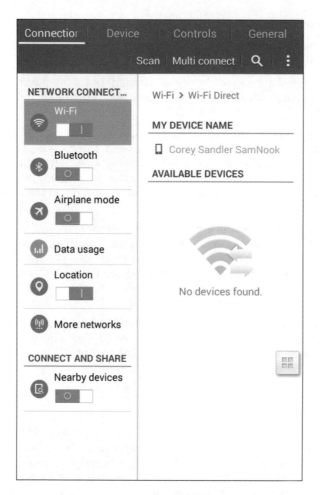

Figure 5-2: If there were a usable Wi-Fi Direct connection, my Samsung Galaxy Tab 4 NOOK (which I call Corey Sandler SamNook) would post details in the Available Devices panel shown here.

Here's what I can tell you, though: When the software catches up with the hardware, you'll be able to communicate from device to device as simply as you can with standard Wi-Fi.

Here's how to turn on Wi-Fi Direct:

1. **Swipe down from the top to display the notification panel.**

2. **Tap the Settings (gear) icon.**

3. **If it isn't already selected, choose the Connections tab.**

4. **If it isn't already on, slide the Wi-Fi switch to the right.**

5. **Tap the Wi-Fi Direct button in the upper-right corner of the screen.**

   The tablet starts scanning for a usable direction wireless connection. Available devices are listed onscreen. If you want to connect to more than one at a time (another advanced technology not yet fully supported), tap Multi Connect in the upper right.

   To disconnect from Wi-Fi Direct, tap End Connection or slide the Wi-Fi switch to the Off position.

King Bluetooth Lives

Another technology for direct wireless connection of devices is Bluetooth. It connects devices at a maximum distance of about 30 feet for simple tasks, a process called *pairing*. On the Tab 4 NOOK, you can use the Bluetooth radio to share photos, contacts, music, and other files. See Figure 5-3.

The technology is, of course, named after Harald Bluetooth, the tenth-century king who united ragtag Danish tribes into a single kingdom, apparently with the aid of a wireless tablet of some sort. True — at least the name part.

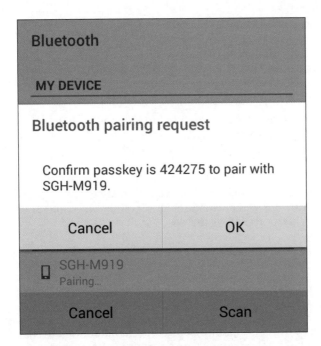

Figure 5-3: The Tab 4 NOOK is asked to confirm a pairing with an SGH-M919, the Samsung model number for one of its advanced smartphones.

To protect your tablet from receiving unwanted pairing requests, don't let it be found by other devices until you agree to let it be discovered.

Understanding Bluetooth

Here's how to establish a Bluetooth pairing. These steps deal with turning on the Bluetooth radio in the Tab 4 NOOK; make sure the equivalent radio is turned on and made *discoverable* on the other device.

Take these steps on the Tab 4 NOOK:

1. **Swipe down from the top to display the notification panel.**

2. **Tap the Bluetooth (angular B) icon to turn on the radio.**

   A menu appears.

3. **Under the My Device section, you should see the name you gave your tablet.**

4. **Tap to place a check mark in Tap to Make Visible to Other Devices option.**

   On some systems this is called making a device *discoverable.* See Figure 5-4.

5. **Look in the Paired Devices section.**

6. **Take the steps according to your Bluetooth history:**

   • For a *previously paired Tab 4 NOOK,* the other device should be listed there; if the system has discovered a new device, tap it to initiate a connection.

   • For a *previously unpaired Tab 4 NOOK,* look for the security code on your tablet's screen. Make sure it's the same on the other device, and tap your approval on each.

When you're finished with a Bluetooth session, simply turn off the Bluetooth radio or the device. From this point forward, because you have established *pairing,* the two devices will automatically reconnect anytime both are within range and their Bluetooth radios are on.

Bluetooth radios use a lot of battery power. Turn off that function when you aren't using it.

Bluetooth limitations

Once again, the hardware capabilities of your Samsung Galaxy Tab 4 NOOK may not be equaled by the software or operating system on your tablet or on a computer or other device to which you connect.

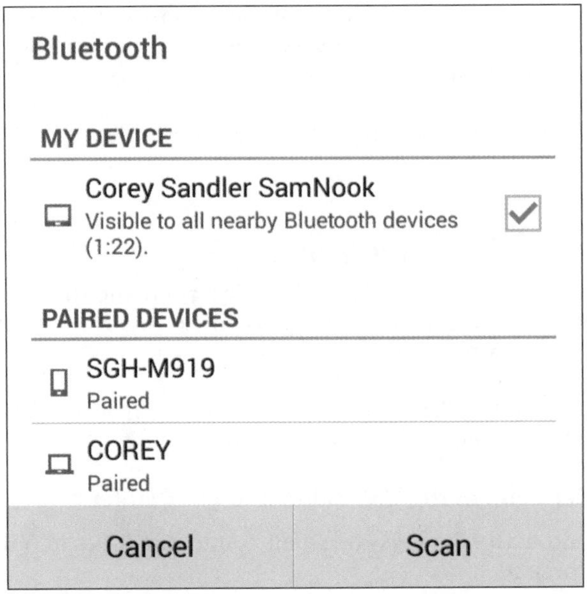

Bluetooth

MY DEVICE

Corey Sandler SamNook
Visible to all nearby Bluetooth devices
(1:22).   ✓

PAIRED DEVICES

SGH-M919
Paired

COREY
Paired

Cancel   Scan

Figure 5-4: Success! Corey Sandler SamNook is paired with
two devices: a Samsung smartphone and a desktop PC, each
of which has a Bluetooth radio.

Some but not all computers, smartphones, or other devices let you transfer
files in either direction with a tablet. Check the settings of Windows, Android,
Apple's OS X on its computers, or Apple's iOS on mobile devices to see
what's allowed.

I could write a sentence here that says transferring files using Bluetooth is
easy-peasy anywhere, anytime, and in any combination of devices. But that
would be wrong. In fact, I recommend using Bluetooth only for simple tasks
like beaming music to an external speaker or headset.

You can usually find a way to perform certain other tasks like syncing contact, calendar, and task information from one device to another, but in truth
I think you'll find Wi-Fi or direct USB cable connection much simpler and
easier for transfer of files.

Getting Physical: USB and Memory Cards

This section steps away from wireless communication and details actual
physical contact for data transfer. I'm calling it *part one if by wire, and two if
by microSDHC card.*

To me, the simplest way to transfer a bunch or files from a desktop or computer to your tablet, and the simplest way to manage files on your tablet, is to use a USB cable between the two devices.

You can use the same USB cable that connects your tablet to its AC adapter for recharging to move data.

Making the USB connection

USB (Universal Serial Bus) is, simply said, a wiring scheme that carries data and electrical power. About the only thing you need to know is which end is up, and which end is micro.

The USB cable that came with your tablet is standard. If you need a replacement, you can get one from a computer store or an online seller.

1. **Plug the micro end of the USB cable into your tablet.**

   The *micro* end of the cable is the small connector. It fits in only in one way. Don't force it.

2. **Remove the larger end of the cable from the AC adapter.**

3. **Put the small adapter somewhere where you'll be able to find it again.**

4. **Attach the larger end of the USB cable to a port on your current desktop or laptop computer.**

   It, too, only goes in a particular way. At the computer end, you need to match the open side of the connector to the block side on the port. Open to block; block to open and you're in like Flynn.

   If you're one of the lucky ones, that's all that needs be done. If not, you should see a message on your computer (not on the tablet) telling you that it needs to install a driver in order to recognize this new piece of hardware now attached. The computer should be able to do this all by itself. If you run into trouble, call Samsung or Barnes & Noble for help.

   When you make the USB connection, you should see a message on your tablet. For a closer look, swipe down from the top to display the notification panel.

5. **Tap the Media Device option (as shown in Figure 5-5).**

   This option is best for moving files to or from your Tab 4 NOOK. Mac users may need to install a small, free utility on their computer.

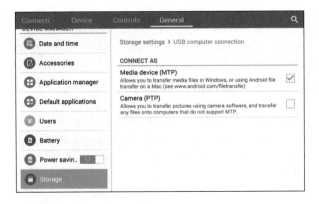

Figure 5-5: Use the Media Device option if you can.

6. **Find your tablet in the File Explorer (on the PC) or the Finder (on a Mac).**

   Mine is called Corey Sandler SamNook.

7. **On the computer, click to open the tablet.**

   You'll find one top level for the tablet and one for the card you may have (should have) installed in the expansion slot.

   On a Windows machine, you can right-click a folder or virtual drive to read more about its properties and how much data is stored within. See Figure 5-6. You might see the tablet referred to by its model number; the first edition of the Samsung Galaxy Tab 4 NOOK is the SM-T230NU.

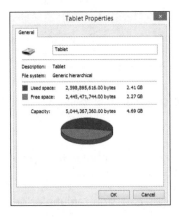 

Figure 5-6: On the left, the Tab 4 NOOK internal storage is displayed on a Windows 8 machine. On the right, its memory card properties.

TIP

If you're going to add files *from* the PC to the tablet, in most cases you will want to install them on the card; it has more space. You can create any folder you want; I suggest leaving the folder names of the device alone. Create new ones on the external memory card instead.

The Android operating system organizes itself based on file type:

- ✔ Any PNG or JPG file goes in the Gallery.

- ✔ Photos you take with your tablet's built-in camera are stored in the DCIM folder. Other folder names are more obvious: Music, Movies, Documents. See Figure 5-7.

- ✔ NOOK eBooks are stored in the NOOK folder.

- ✔ Files you've downloaded to the tablet are in Downloads.

- ✔ Files created using some apps are in Documents.

- ✔ Some apps create their own folders, including Overdrive for library books and Kindle for reading material from Amazon's store.

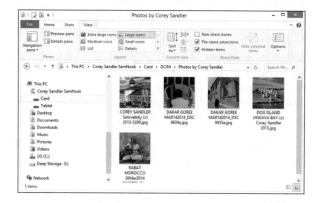

Figure 5-7: I used the USB cable to transfer photos. I stored them in a new folder that I placed within the DCIM folder on the tablet's memory card.

Use the same basic file operations of the computer to copy or move files from one device to the other, in either direction. You can

- ✔ Open a folder on the tablet or its card and rename or delete files.

- ✔ Drag and drop files from the PC to the tablet, or the other direction.

✔ Copy files on a PC or Mac, move the cursor to a folder on the tablet, and paste them there.

✔ Drag and drop entire folders in one direction or the other.

Check out the basic file structure of the tablet itself in Figure 5-8.

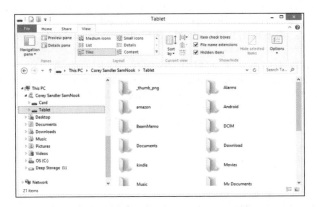

Figure 5-8: From my computer, here's my Tab 4 NOOK internal memory file structure. Some folders are standard; some (like Amazon) were added by apps I installed on my tablet.

If you're connecting your Tab 4 NOOK to a Macintosh computer, you must eject the tablet's Disk icon before you can turn off USB storage on the Tab and remove the cable. Windows users can simply unplug the cable without any extra steps.

It's in the cards

One more way to transfer data to and from your tablet is to treat the microSDHC card as if it were a floppy disk. You can remove the tiny sliver of memory from its slot on the side of the Tab 4 NOOK and bring it to a desktop or laptop computer and install it there.

After installing the card, use the same drag-and-drop or copy and paste techniques you'd use if your tablet were connected to a computer by the USB cable.

You can attach a microSDHC card to a computer two ways:

✔ **Insert it into the slot in your laptop/computer that accepts the card.** Be sure to match the type and size of card to the proper slot.

If your computer has a slot for the larger (matchbook-sized) SD card, you can use a microSDHC-to-SD converter; you may have received one with your microSDHC card when you purchased it. Slide the micro version into the larger converter and then plug the converter into your computer.

✔ **Buy an external memory card reader that accepts various card sizes.** Make sure it works with your microSDHC either directly or indirectly. You may need to use a converter, as discussed in the previous method. Card readers plug into a standard USB port on your laptop or desktop.

Be careful handling the somewhat fragile microSDHC memory card and don't touch the gold contacts. Also, properly eject or unmount the microSDHC card from the computer before physically removing it. If you don't know the procedure on your particular computer, shut down the entire computer in the normal way and then remove the microSDHC card.

Sending Air Mail

Email and the cloud are two last means of transferring files to and from your tablet. They both require an active Wi-Fi connection.

Sending yourself email

You can send or receive emails with attachments and then download the files for storage. For example, to move a copy of a photo or a text file from your desktop to your tablet, do this:

1. **Send yourself an email with the files attached.**

2. **Open the email on your tablet and download the files.**

3. **Later, use a file manager to move the file from the Downloads folder to another folder within the device or on the memory card.**

The same process works the other direction. Send files from your tablet to yourself, and open the email on your desktop or laptop computer. That's how I transferred most of the screenshots you see in this book: grab a shot, go to the gallery, and share the image by email.

Using the cloud

Another solution, especially good for large files, is the cloud. What do we mean by the *cloud?* It's a storage system that exists out on the Internet — anywhere — that you can get to with your tablet. You use it for uploading and downloading files. It exists as a storage place of its own, not directly attached to your tablet or computer.

One of the beauties of this sort of system is that it is (to use an old computer word) *asynchronous.* Both sides of the equation don't need to be online or connected at the same time.

Dropbox is an example. It offers a free trial subscription to buyers of the Galaxy Tab 4 NOOK. Another example is Microsoft's SkyDrive, which offers free storage and services. You may well be able to get by with the basic amount of storage, or you can buy more.

To use these services, you either reach them using an app on your tablet, or use the web browser to reach their site from a tablet or a computer. After logging in with a password, you upload files to the site or download ones already stored there.

I use this sort of service to store a full set of my most important files when I travel. In that way, if my tablet or smartphone or laptop fails or otherwise goes missing, I can always sign in from someone else's device or from a replacement. Be sure to use a secure password to protect any sensitive material you store in the cloud.

6

Putting in Your Contacts

*I*t's taken a long, long time but I am finally getting my social and business affairs organized. I still have a gigantic Rolodex of business cards I collected decades ago. My desktop is littered with scraps of paper with notes about people I have met or worked with. Don't even get me started about the file cabinets in my office; some have not been opened since the previous millennium.

But the concept that finally got me de-scattered is *synchronization.* It lets you connect the dots on all of those scraps of information, merging information from desktop and laptop computers, tablets, and smartphones.

Just about everything can become connected. Take a picture with the camera and tag a buddy; that image goes to your list of contacts. Get an email or message from that person, and his or her picture appears along with the text. It works the other direction as well: Use the information in your contacts to easily send someone a book excerpt or a recommendation.

Just recently I realized that the color of my desktop is black. All of those scraps of paper — well, nearly all of them — have gone to that great recycling bin in the sky.

Roaming Friends and Countrymen

If you've previously set up and used a Google account, you likely have a list of friends and acquaintances. When you link your new Tab 4 NOOK to that same Google account, those contacts come right over to your tablet.

Your contacts can include your social networking app friends and, with a little bit of fancy electronic footwork, you can *import* (bring to your tablet) information from other sources, like Microsoft Outlook and Apple Contacts and iCloud.

TIP

If you want to import contacts from a source other than Google, Samsung, or Barnes & Noble, check the Play Store on the Tab 4 NOOK to see if there's an app to do this for you. For example, Microsoft's Outlook app lets you import contacts and calendar items from that service to the Android equivalents on your tablet, and keep each side in sync with the other; a change to the details of a contact in one is reflected in the other.

Take a look at the contact in Figure 6-1.

Figure 6-1: This contact's name, email, and numbers have all been replaced with fakes by me, her father, so leave her alone. She gets enough mail and calls already.

If you haven't yet set up a Google or Samsung account, go to the app on your tablet for those two companies to do so. You can also set up an Outlook account by using the web browser and searching for that Microsoft site.

Everything but the Kitchen Sync

Your tablet can *synchronize* with many different accounts, so if you change an email address on your tablet, that change is reflected on other devices, too.

Be careful about what sorts of information you share; assume that anything — and I mean anything — can and will be used against you in a court of marketing or worse.

Figure 6-2 shows other accounts that can merge their information into your tablet, or which can get information from your Tab 4 NOOK:

- ✔ **Samsung account.** You may not even know you have one, but if you signed up for a Samsung account when you were setting up your tablet, or if you did so for another Samsung device like a smartphone, you're in.

- ✔ **Google account.** They may not yet own the world, but they're on their way. Do you have an account for Gmail or YouTube? That counts.

- ✔ **Microsoft Exchange ActiveSync.** Businesses, organizations, and some Internet providers use this to synchronize email, contacts, calendar listings and other live data.

- ✔ **LDAP (Lightweight Directory Access Protocol).** Some businesses and web services use this service to organize directories.

- ✔ **Facebook and Twitter.** If you've got an account with these folks, your information — including your friends and their contact information — can be shared with your tablet.

If you already use Gmail and other Google apps, your contacts there automatically sync with your new Galaxy Tab 4 NOOK, provided that you use the same username. Just associate your NOOK with the Google account and you're good to go.

Creating a contact by hand

About that stack of business cards I collected on my most recent trip: I just might want to add some of them as contacts. I'm sure that was the intent of the person who gave it to me.

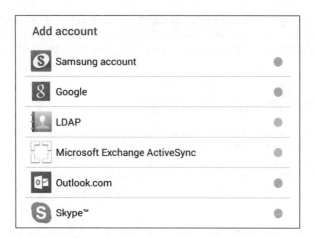

Figure 6-2: You can add accounts as sources for contacts from half a dozen or more sources.

Here's how to digitally (using your own digits) create a contact:

1. **Open the Contacts app.**

   You can open the Apps menu and look for the orange outline of a head labeled Contacts and tap that. Or you may have set a Contacts shortcut on one of the Home screens.

   You'll most likely see the listing for "Me" at the top of a panel on the left. That's Me as in You, created automatically for you. The one on my tablet has me, unless I am you, which is not likely. If you want to add more information to Me, tap Set Up Profile.

2. **Tap the + icon at the top of the screen.**

3. **Choose where to save the contact:**

   • **Device.** That's your tablet. If you choose this option, the contact is saved only on your Tab 4 NOOK and not automatically made available for sharing with other listings.

   • **Google.** The contact is synced with your online Google account. Not only does this create a backup copy of your contact, but it lets other Android devices (such as a smartphone or another tablet) have access to the contact.

   • **Samsung Account.** The contact is synced with the listing maintained by that company and available on other devices from Samsung, including a smartphone or another tablet.

- **Add a New Account.** You can add a Microsoft Exchange ActiveSync account. The problem is, if you import from this sort of account and then merge the results into your Android contacts list, the information's not protected by the cocoon of security at its original location.

In a perfect world, I'd recommend the Google account. Think twice about what information you share, use a tough password to protect your accounts, and change that password often. Oh, and best of luck.

After you select a place to store your new contact, the Create Contact form opens.

4. **Tap text fields on the Add Contact screen and fill in information.**

That includes name, phone numbers, and email addresses. See Figure 6-3. Where offered, tap the down arrow to see more fields.

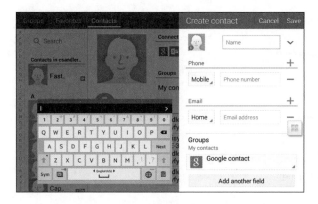

Figure 6-3: You can add or remove fields. (I used the floating keyboard to make the screen easier to see; see Chapter 3).

If you want to tidy up the contact to remove empty text fields, tap the red – (minus) button.

You can

- Assign a contact to an existing group, like Family or Friends.
- Create your own group, like a Human Chess Players Federation group.
- Tap Add Another Field for more options.
- Add notes or a field for a person's nickname. See Figure 6-4.

To add a photo to the listing, follow these steps:

1. **Tap the blank picture space at the top of the contact.**

   It has a plus symbol on it.

2. **Tap to select a photo from your tablet's Gallery.**

   If the person whose contact you're creating is right in front of you, tap Take Picture to use the tablet's built-in camera.

3. **Crop the picture with the provided tool, if it's available.**

   The box is square, while nearly all images are rectangular. Something has to give.

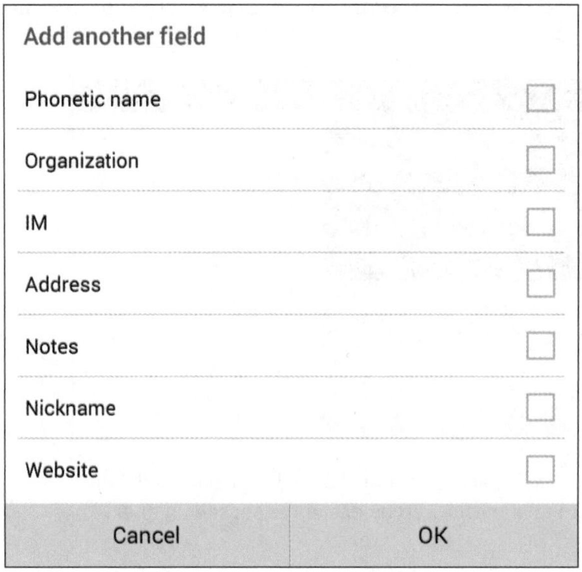

Add another field	
Phonetic name	☐
Organization	☐
IM	☐
Address	☐
Notes	☐
Nickname	☐
Website	☐
Cancel	OK

Figure 6-4: I add a Notes field to help me personalize my emails or track recent events.

Importing contacts from a computer

You can also *migrate* (to use a geekish term) your collection of names, addresses, and email addresses from your desktop or laptop PC or Mac *to* the Tab 4 NOOK.

The trick is this: *Export* your contacts list from the computer in a compatible format that can be *imported* into the Tab 4 NOOK. Not just any format will work. See Figure 6-5.

Import/Export contacts
Import from USB storage
Export to USB storage
Import from SD card
Export to SD card

Figure 6-5: Import/export connects by USB cable, or uses files on the microSDHC card in your tablet.

1. **Open your email or contacts program on your computer and look for a command to export records.**

   It may be under the File menu item. If you can, go ahead and export your contacts as vCards to a location on your computer.

   If you're lucky, you will find an option to export the files as *vCard* files, or in the VCF file format. This option is available on the Mac and on certain mail programs on Windows machines including Windows Mail and Windows Live Mail. It is *not* available in the widely used Outlook program on Windows machines.

2. **Connect the Samsung Galaxy Tab 4 NOOK to the computer using the USB cable.**

3. **Transfer contacts to the tablet.**

   You can put the file anywhere; when you're done, you can delete the VCF file from your tablet because it'll have converted them to an Android style.

4. **With the files on the Galaxy Tab, open the Contacts app on your tablet.**

5. **Choose the Import/Export command.**

6. **Choose Import from SD Card.**

7. **In the Save Contact To option, tap Phone.**

   Yes, we both know the Tab 4 NOOK is a tablet, not a phone, but the Android operating system was developed for smartphones first and is not always consistent in its menu options.

   You may end up with some duplicate Contacts entries. You can handle that later by joining multiple contacts; I deal with that later in this chapter.

Importing contacts through Gmail

Another way to get contacts from a computer onto your tablet is to use an intermediate web-based service, like Google's Gmail. This is one way to deal with computer programs like Outlook that don't produce vCards.

The process here is to export files as a CSV file (known to propeller-heads as a comma-separated values file), which is basically a set of details in a particular order separated by commas. Something like: Corey, Sandler, 508-555-0199,corey@notmyrealaddress.com. No, that isn't my real phone number. It's a certified phony number in the 555-01xx range maintained by telephone companies for use in movies, songs, and books. "We're sorry. Your call cannot be completed."

Grouping and Degrouping Contacts

If you've only got a handful of contacts, you can just leave them in a single short list. And then you should get out more and meet some new people.

Once your collection grows to many dozens, you can make some contacts members of a group, or make some of them favorites. Here's how to categorize:

1. **Open the Contacts app.**

2. **Tap the Groups tab.**

3. **Create your own group and assign contacts to it.**

   Or, choose from pre-labeled groups such as Family, Friends, Co-workers. The Not Assigned group is actually a group, as opposed to contacts which haven't been assigned to a group, if you get my meaning.

   To add a single contact to a group, simply edit the Group field for that contact.

Cooking up multiple group contacts

You can add group members by the dozen, or the baker's dozen, if you like. Here's how:

1. **Tap Contacts, then tap Groups.**

2. **Tap the group you want to use.**

3. **Tap Menu, then choose Add Member.**

   Contacts that are available for categorization will be displayed.

4. **Tap the name of each contact to add, or tap Select All.**

5. **Tap Done to add the contacts to the group.**

The fifth Beatle: Removing group members

Sometimes it's time to thin the herd. Here's how to remove some or all members of a group:

1. **Tap Contacts and then tap Groups.**

2. **Tap the group from which you want to remove members.**

3. **Tap Menu. Then tap Remove Member.**

4. **Tap the name of each contact to be removed, or tap Select All.**

5. **Tap Done to remove the contact(s).**

Renaming a group

And when time comes to change the name of a group, you can do that, too:

1. **Tap Contacts, and then tap Groups.**

2. **Tap the group you want to rename.**

3. **Tap Menu, then tap Edit Group.**

4. **Tap the group Name field and type a new name.**

5. **Tap Save to seal the deal.**

Deleting a group

The end comes for all, including some groups on a Tab 4 NOOK. Here's how to be rid of one or more:

1. **Tap Contacts, then Groups, then Menu. Then tap Delete Groups.**

2. **Tap the names of groups you want to delete, or tap Select All.**

3. **Tap Done to complete your order.**

4. **Tap Group Only to delete the group name.**

   Or, tap Group and Group Members to send both the group and all of its members to the digital dumpster.

Playing Favorites with Contacts

We all play favorites, whether we admit it or not. You don't have to admit it, but you can apply a favorite designation to as many of your contacts as you want.

How does a Favorite differ from assigning a contact to a group? Favorites can extend across multiple groups, and can be made up of only some of the members of a group, or include people who aren't in a group of any kind. But when it comes time to send out a "Party time!" email, or any other sort of major announcement to a select group, you can blast it out to your chosen favorites. See Figure 6-6.

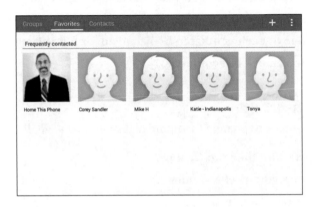

Figure 6-6: You can see contacts as members of groups, those marked as favorites, or (here) those you've recently or frequently contacted.

Marking a contact as a favorite

Shush. It's our little secret, okay? It's so easy you don't even need to edit the listing. Here's how you give a contact a golden star as a favorite:

1. **Tap Contacts.**

2. **Tap the contact you want to honor with the favorite distinction.**

3. **Tap the grayed-out star and turn it gold with pride.**

Viewing contacts marked as favorites

To see your secret list of favorites, do this:

1. **Tap Contacts.**

2. **Tap the Favorites tab.**

    You'll see only those contacts with the golden star.

Removing a favorite from a contact

Sometimes things just don't work out. Was it something I said? Were you politically incorrect? Maybe it was the shoes. Here's how to take away a single gold star or a whole phalanx of them:

1. **Tap Contacts and then tap Favorites.**

2. **Tap Menu, then choose Remove from Favorites.**

3. **Tap an individual contact or tap Select All.**

4. **Tap Done to complete the process.**

Managing Your Contacts

Much of the time, your contacts sit quietly in the background, providing information when you need it to fill out an email address line, send a photo, or communicate about books from the eReader.

But to go directly to your contacts to examine, add, delete, or edit listings, do this:

1. **From the Home screen, tap the Apps icon.**

2. **Tap the Contacts icon (a little orange head).**

   You can place a shortcut to Contacts on one of the Home screen panels.

You can easily end up with a huge number of contacts, and good for you. My theory is: when in doubt, add a contact. You can always delete, edit, or merge *(link)* later.

Not every contact has a picture, and the picture can come from any of the sources of information you are tapping to construct the list. For example, if you have a photo assigned within your Gmail account, that photo will come along with the address, email, and phone number to your tablet.

The standard way Contacts are sorted is alphabetically by last name. Within that section, they are sorted with first name first. So, under L you will find Abraham Lincoln ahead of Robert Todd Lincoln with Mary Todd Lincoln in between. Scroll through by swiping your finger, or jump to someone by tapping a letter.

Changing the order

If you're the sort of person who likes to keep track of your contacts based on their first names, your Tab 4 NOOK can do that, too. See Figure 6-7. Here's how to change the sorting order:

1. **Start the Contacts app.**

2. **Tap the Menu icon in the upper right.**

3. **Choose Settings.**

4. **Tap List By.**

5. **Tap First Name or Last Name.**

6. **Press the Back key to exit.**

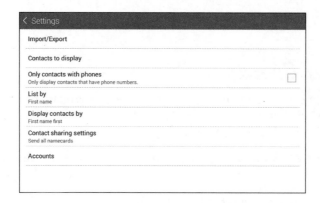

Figure 6-7: Tap List By (in Settings) to choose between sorting by first or last name.

Editing or deleting a contact

Things change. This is something I've learned from a relatively long (thus far) and sometimes confusing life. And so you may need to edit (see Figure 6-8) or even delete an existing contact. Here's how:

1. **Open the Contacts app.**

2. **Tap the contact in need of rectification.**

3. **Tap the Edit (pencil) icon.**

4. **Tap the text field you want to change.**

   Use the onscreen keyboard to make changes.

Or do this:

1. **Tap the trash can icon.**

2. **Tap OK to confirm you really want to make the contact go away.**

   If this contact is synced to Google or other online accounts, deleting it on your tablet also deletes it from anywhere else it resides.

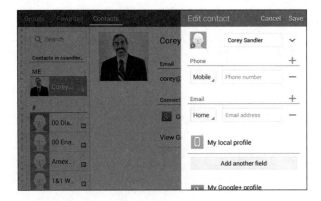

Figure 6-8: Open an existing contact and edit any field.

Sending Email from Your Contacts

Since the Samsung Galaxy Tab 4 NOOK is a Wi-Fi device without a cellular phone connection, it lacks standard phone facilities. The primary means of communication from the tablet is email.

You can start an email from your contacts list:

1. **From the Contacts app, tap a contact.**

   You see a contact name.

2. **Tap an email address and you (and the contact's address) will be ready for use.**

   If a contact has more than one email address, select the one you want to use.

3. **Tap an email option.**

   The Tab 4 NOOK is set up to send email through Gmail. When I added the Outlook.com app to my tablet, that choice began appearing as a mail option. See Figure 6-9.

4. **Type your message.**

   A different way to send an email is to choose the contact and tap the Menu icon in the upper right. Then tap Send Email.

And, as you see in Chapter 7 about Email, you don't have to start the process in Contacts. You can open a page to send an email and type in a name; the tablet will hunt in Contacts for the address.

Figure 6-9: If you tap an email listing, you can send a message using one of the email accounts.

Linking Duplicate Contacts

It's quite easy to end up with two, four, six, or more duplicate entries in your Contacts listings. You might have made an entry for your friend Jack Smith under "Smith, Jack" and "Jack Smith" and "John Smith," for example. Or you might have identical name entries but differing email or phone information in each.

Because the Galaxy Tab 4 NOOK can grab contacts from Google and Samsung and Facebook and Twitter and more, dupes are quite common. See Figure 6-10.

Figure 6-10: I found five entries for one ferry service, built up over the years on different accounts.

Your first option is to go to Contacts and edit or delete duplicates or outdated entries. Or you can *link* entries so all the information is brought together in one place. Here's how:

1. **Open the Contacts list.**

2. **Open a contact that has duplicate entries.**

The Connection section tells you the source of that entry.

3. **In the Connection section, tap the link (chain) icon.**

4. **Tap Link Another Contact (at the bottom).**

   The tablet sees if it can determine a likely duplicate and lists it under Suggestions.

5. **Tap a duplicate entry to link it to the original. See Figure 6-11.**

6. **If necessary, tap Link Another Contact again, and make further links.**

   You can link as many as ten entries.

7. **Press the Back key when you're done linking.**

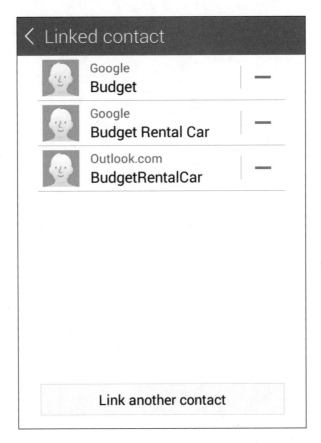

Figure 6-11: A successful linkage of three listings from two sources for one car rental company.

7

We've All Got Email

*Y*ou've got an eReader that can play videos, sing songs, and take dictation. It isn't surprising that it can also send and receive messages to and from anyone with an email address. And, of course, that includes just about everyone you know. For the majority of users, email setup will be automatic.

Hey Mister Postman

The Galaxy Tab 4 NOOK comes to you with two email apps: Email (part of the Android operating system) and Gmail (a web-based service that also comes from Google.) You can also add others, like Outlook.com and Yahoo Mail.

In this chapter, I concentrate on the Email app, which is quite full featured. You can even make it go out and get email from sources including most of the major brand names as well as from private domains. What's a *private domain?* Say you run a business and have your own website; you might just accept email through that address. Something like corey@this_is_not_my_address.com, which as you might imagine, is not my address but an example of a domain.

Writing Home about the Email App

You may have already set up your email particulars when you set up your tablet. In that case, you might want to skip a bit of this chapter and explore the process of reading and sending mail and customization options. The rest of you might want to start by setting up a new email account.

The Email app is right there on your Home screen. You can also find it if you open the Apps panel. Look for the icon with an envelope sealed with a red @ sign. Tap the icon to see the inbox. Mine is shown in Figure 7-1.

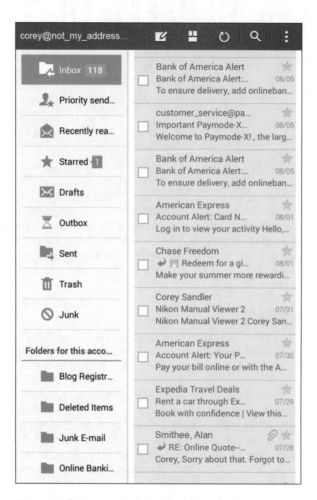

Figure 7-1: Folders on the left side and received messages on the right.

The Email app exists on your tablet. Using a tablet-based app allows you to read, write, and manage (but not send or receive) email even if you don't have a Wi-Fi signal.

Setting up an email account, automatic style

If you already have an email account with one of the major providers — Gmail, Yahoo, Outlook, AOL, many Internet providers — you'll probably be able to add that account to your tablet with just a few bits of information. The Email app already knows the standard settings for them.

1. **Tap the Email icon to open the app.**

2. **To create a new account, tap the Menu icon in the upper-right corner.**

3. **Tap Settings.**

   You see a screen with a panel on the left side with two sections: General and Account Settings.

4. **In the Account Settings section, tap + Add Account.**

5. **Enter your existing email account and password. See Figure 7-2.**

6. **Tap Done.**

   The Email app churns away, making contact with Google and attempting to communicate with the email provider you use. (The name of the provider is usually the second half of your address, called the *domain*. For example, econo1@aol.com is an address at the old-school provider AOL.

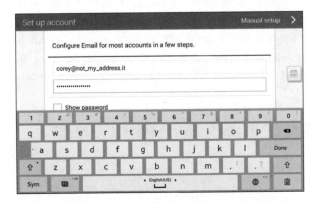

Figure 7-2: Both automatic and manual setup for email accounts begin with entering the address and password.

Setting up an email account, manual style

On the other hand, if you have your own domain or use a less-popular email provider, you may have to go through the manual setup process. I'm not talking about assembling the Space Shuttle from a box of parts here, so no worries.

You have two relatively painless ways to manually set up an email account:

- ✔ With the Email app open to the Manual Setup screen, call your Internet provider. Ask them to help fill in the missing blanks for incoming and outgoing servers, plus any security scheme they use.

- ✔ Open the email program on the computer or smartphone that already gets email from this provider. All the information you need is on the Setup screen for the existing account.

In general, don't expect much help here from NOOK or Samsung. But you might find a kindly technician who will help you get the information you need from your computer or a smartphone that already uses the account.

Here's how to proceed *after* you get the information:

1. **Follow Steps 1 through 6 in the automatic style section just before this.**

   You'll be taken to a screen that asks, "What type of account?" See Figure 7-3.

2. **Tap an option:**

   - **POP3.** Delivers messages from the email server onto your local computer, which may not be the best option for mobile devices. And if you lose your tablet, you could lose all unarchived email.

   - **IMAP.** Works well with folders and mobile devices. Leaves the original messages on the email server, downloading a copy to your tablet.

   - **Microsoft Exchange ActiveSync.** If you use this option, sometimes referred to as an EAS account, contact the systems manager for details.

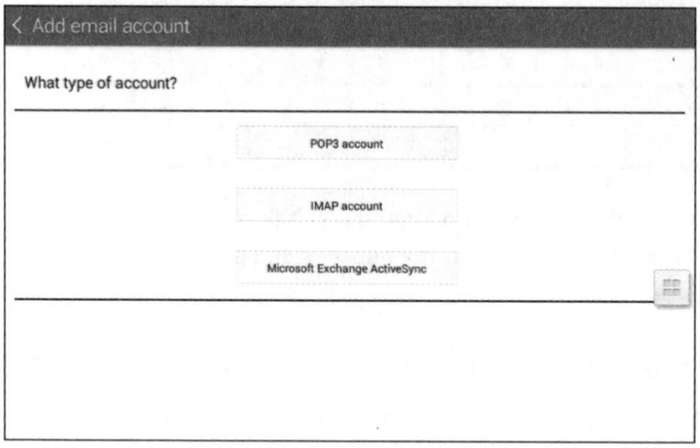

Figure 7-3: The Email app works with three common email acronyms and the protocols behind them: POP3, IMAP, and EAS.

Use the standard keyboard to enter passwords. Don't swipe or use dictation.

3. **Type server settings for the incoming server (the system that delivers mail to you).**

   Re-enter the username and password, and then enter the name of the IMAP server, usually in the form imap.*servername*.com. Get this information from the email provider or from your desktop or laptop computer already configured to use this account.

4. **Choose a security type from the menu.**

   Follow the same specifications that your email provider gave you. Some use none, others may demand SSL or TLS.

   Most email services use standard ports on your tablet (think of them as entrance and exit ramps from a superhighway). Check to see if your provider wants you to use a port other than the suggested one.

   The Outgoing Settings dialog box opens, as shown in Figure 7-4.

Figure 7-4: Part of the configuration panel for outgoing settings of an IMAP account.

5. **Enter the address for the SMTP server.**

   It's usually in the form smtp.*servername*.com. This server distributes your outgoing mail to the Internet.

6. **Enter a security type, if required, and check that the proper port is chosen.**

7. **Tap Done.**

   If all goes well, you're taken to the incoming mail panel and can see the account you added. If there's a problem, check all the settings against the ones you use on your computer or smartphone, or call the provider for assistance.

Customizing Your General Email Settings

There are a dizzying number of ways you can customize your email account. Some are more important for all users, a few are important only to a few. But they're all there.

The following sections describe what you find in General Settings. You can get there from the Email app: Tap the Menu icon in the upper right corner and then tap Settings.

Display options

These settings relate to how the Email app works for all accounts:

- **Auto Fit Content.** You can shrink email content to fit the screen; you can still zoom in on the details. I don't much like this option on the relatively small screen of the Tab 4 NOOK; imagine how difficult this would be on an even smaller smartphone.

- **Display.** You can customize the message preview line (none, 1, 2, or 3 lines) that gives you a hint of what lies beneath the summary of an incoming email.

- **Title Line in List.** You can see the sender's name, or the title or subject of the message at the top of each received email listed.

Composing and sending options

To get to this section, you have to be in the Email app: Tap the Menu icon in the upper right corner and then tap Settings.

- **Quick Responses.** Here you can edit some prewritten responses you might want to use in emails. Standard ones include the all-time favorite, "I am out of the office. I will respond to your email as soon as possible on my return." Although you might be tempted to add some rude canned responses, I suggest resisting; sooner or later you'll regret having them available. See Figure 7-5.

- **Default Image Size.** Set the default size for images you attach to emails.

- **Delay Email Sending.** Here's an option that you might want to consider using. Turn on this option to have the tablet wait a few seconds (you choose how many) after you press Send before it actually puts it out on the Internet. Think of it as an Oops button, or perhaps a Wait While I Cool Down button. You can cancel a message that's in this delay period.

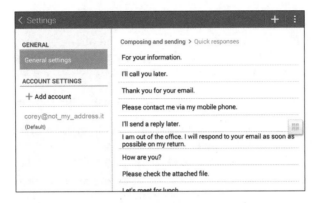

Figure 7-5: You can insert a canned response into an email. You can also add your own. Carefully.

- **Auto Advance Options.** What do you want the tablet to do after you delete, move, forward, or otherwise finish with an email? There's just one set of choices: Go to the next email, the previous email, or the entire list of emails.

- **Confirm Deletions.** Do you want the system to ask you to confirm that you really, really do want to delete a message? Then place a check mark in this box.

- **Priority Senders.** All friends and family are created equal, but some are more equal than others. You can designate certain senders as Priority; their messages go into the Priority Sender inbox.

  You can make the Priority Sender inbox the one you go to when you open the Email app. You can also turn on or off onscreen notifications when certain email comes in, and apply a special ringtone for the most favored.

- **Spam Addresses and Rules for Filtering.** Although it's to some extent like pushing a string up a hill, you can mark certain senders as spammers and place their addresses in a special folder. Tap this option to edit the list of spammers. You can also set up rules that filter certain types of messages directly into your spam folder. The problem here is that some legitimate email will be tagged as spam, and most spammers are fiendishly clever at getting around spam filters with adumbrations and circumlocutions, otherwise known as fancy and misleading words.

The Email app can handle many email accounts. That way you can see all of your mail in one place. The app's left panel has a Combined View option, which brings together all mail from all sources rather than requiring you to look at each account separately.

Customizing settings for specific accounts

On the Email app's Settings panel, tap the name of one of your accounts to customize more settings *just for that account.* Note that in the upper right you'll see Delete Account. Don't touch, unless you want to delete that account.

Here are the other settings — enough to fill two entire panels:

✔ **Sync Settings.** First of all, if you want the email server to send you messages anytime you're on a Wi-Fi connection, turn on Sync Email. Without that check mark, the only time you'll get emails is when you load the app.

After then, you can make all sorts of adjustments to the sync schedule, even to the point of having different time periods and urgencies for working hours and whatever you call the rest of your day.

✔ **Signature.** You can have a personalized message at the bottom of every email you send. As delivered, the signature says "Sent from Samsung tablet." I don't send advertising messages unless someone pays me. I use my full name plus my blog and website.

Whatever you put as your signature can be edited on the screen before you send a message, in case you don't want to give the full measure of information to everyone.

✔ **Default Account.** Turn on this option to make this particular account the one that sends all *outgoing* messages, unless you change that setting on the message itself. Only one account can be set as the default.

✔ **Password.** This is a quick way to update your password setting if it has changed on another device.

Notification settings

These settings determine how your device will inform your new messages.

✔ **Email Notifications.** An email's subject can appear in your tablet's notification panel and briefly in the status bar when it arrives.

✔ **Select Ringtone.** Accept the default or choose a different one.

Tap More settings to see more options.

Common settings

I deal here just with the less-than-obvious settings:

✔ **Always Cc/Bcc Myself.** Press here and tap a check mark in Cc or Bcc so that every message you send comes back to you as a copy. Why would you do this? It's one way to make sure your tablet is properly sending and receiving messages; if you don't get your copy, something is wrong. See Figure 7-6.

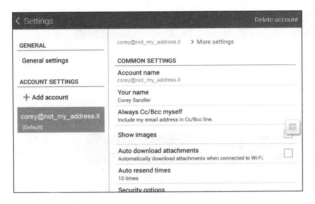

Figure 7-6: Options for specific accounts let you control images, downloads, and certain sending preferences.

Youngsters: *Cc* stands for *carbon copy,* which used to be made by placing a piece of carbon paper under an original in a typewriter or even for handwriting. It was considered proper office etiquette to notify both the primary and secondary recipients that a carbon or duplicate copy of a message had been created and sent. A *Bcc* is a *blind carbon copy,* which was a copy that the original recipient was not told had been made.

✔ **Show Images.** You can download and display all images in received emails. Without the check mark on this option, messages arrive and display quicker, and you're told to tap a button to show images in a message.

✔ **Auto Download Attachments.** When you turn on this option, any attachments are automatically downloaded. If you don't let them automatically download, you have to request it. Automatic download could slow your system and *possibly* expose it to malware, although that hasn't yet proved to be a major problem on Android systems.

Open It Up!

Once you set up the system, most of the not-quite-hard-work has been done. Tap the Email icon to see folders on the left side and mail on the right.

If you have more than one email account on your tablet, tap the menu in the upper left and choose which one to look at, or choose Combined View to bring them all to one place.

Mail that you haven't read yet has a blue first line. If a message has an attachment, you see a paperclip icon. Tap an email to expand it for reading. See Figure 7-7.

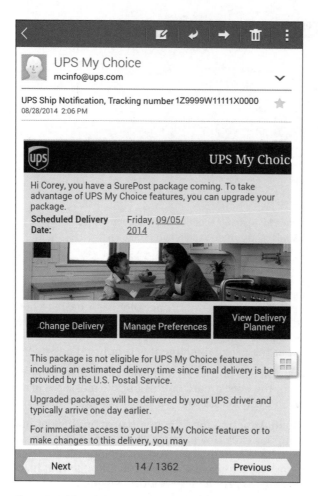

Figure 7-7: Messages like this one that have images may require your permission to download the pictures.
A paint-by-numbers Sistine Chapel replica is my next project.

While you're in the Email app, email is organized by date; tap the Menu icon in the upper right and tap Sort By to change that.

You also see these options:

- ✔ **View As.** You can choose Conversation View, which groups all messages from a single person or address together. The problem here is that most users tend to receive most of their mail from a small number of senders and this could easily divert your attention away from a new and important message from someone else.

- ✔ **Font Size.** You can adjust the size of the type in messages.

Now you're ready to read your mail. Tap any message to display its contents. If there's an attachment, you can see it by tapping the panel.

Email that you've saved, or otherwise haven't sent, is automatically stored in the Draft folder. Tap the Draft folder, and then tap any message within. You can edit it and send it from that folder, or throw it away.

At the top of the message viewing screen you'll see a panel of eight icons. From left to write, they are:

✓ **New Email.** Tap the icon of a pen to write a message. Start by entering the email address. As you begin typing, look at the black banner in the middle of the screen; the tablet tries to match your entry to your contacts. When you see the one you want, tap it.

On the new email form you'll see these icons:

- A paperclip adds an attachment of a text, audio, photo, or other file.

- An X cancels the message.

- A floppy disk means "Save this message as a draft until I retrieve it to send."

- An envelope with an arrow means "Send this message now."

✓ **Preview Panel.** The blocks icon shows how many panels you want to see. Two blocks means message title and date, plus details within a single message. Three blocks show the folder list plus two other panels. You can touch and move the dividers to adjust the size of panels. See Figure 7-8.

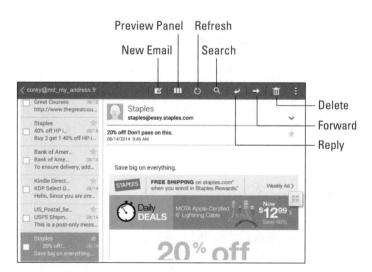

Figure 7-8: In the two-panel email display, I have message titles on the left and the currently selected message at right.

✔ **Refresh.** Tap the circular arrow to sync or refresh the email account.

✔ **Search.** The magnifying glass icon opens a search panel where you can have the tablet hunt for emails based on sender name or a word in its subject.

✔ **Reply.** No need for a stamp. Just tap the leftward arrow to reply to a received message. You'll have room at the top to include a new message, like: "I found this video of a cat in a paper grocery bag and thought of you immediately."

The Original Message option is below the message pane. Tap to remove the check mark if you don't want to re-send the previous message but just want to reply. If there is a check mark, you can tap the panel below to edit the original message.

✔ **Forward.** The right-facing arrow is the means to send a copy of a received message to someone else. You'll need to enter an email address. And you can edit the original message, which is an odd option to offer since that means you're not actually *forwarding* a message but instead sending something new.

✔ **Delete.** Get rid of, toss away, trash. The current message — or all messages from the list where you have placed a check mark in the box — will be moved to the Trash folder.

Email you send to the trash isn't actually erased from your tablet until you go to the Trash folder and select them for final disposal. You can place check marks one by one, or tap the Menu icon in the upper right and tap Delete All.

Starting an Email from Other Apps

Almost every app on your tablet has a Share function. If you're looking at a photo in the Gallery and want to show it a friend, tapping the two-prong Share icon (shown to the left) opens an email message with the picture attached. For example, the NOOK eReader also allows you to share quotes or comments, or to lend certain books. Enter an email address and send it; the Email app does the work in the background without you having to open it.

Getting Attached

You can send and receive files as attachments. For example, you can send a document to someone so she can save it to her tablet or other device. While working on this book, I sent a copy of the incomplete and sometimes incorrect instruction manual for the Tab 4 NOOK from my desktop computer to the tablet. I got the email on my tablet — it was a PDF document that I opened using the Adobe Reader app — and then saved a copy to the Downloads folder for later.

Going the other way, I sent many screen captures from the Tab 4 NOOK to my desktop computer as email attachments.

If you receive an attachment on your tablet, you'll need the proper app to read it. Tap Save to keep a copy of the attachment in the Downloads folder on your tablet's microSDHC card.

Many messages that arrive with an attachment can work with the Preview option to examine them in a small window within the Email app. The Hancom Office suite opens most Microsoft Office word-processing, spreadsheet, and presentation files, for example.

8

Using the Galaxy to Go World Wide (Web)

*T*he Internet machine is a gigantic collection of hissing, dripping pipes and an unfathomably gigantic, messy pile of stuff scattered around just about every nook, NOOK, and cranny of the world.

The amazing tool we use: a *browser*. Your Samsung Galaxy Tab 4 NOOK comes with the Chrome web browser.

Although Chrome is the official browser for the Tab 4 NOOK, you can use any browser that works with a tablet running a current version of the Android operating system: Dolphin, Firefox, and Opera. You can find them at Google's Play Store, the NOOK Shop, and the Samsung store. In my experience, browsers either work or they don't work and they rarely cause problems with other apps on your device; there's no problem with having more than one available on your Tab 4 NOOK.

A browser can take you anywhere on the web. You may find it easier and a bit quicker to use a special-purpose shortcut or app for certain sites. The Tab 4 NOOK comes with apps that go directly to Dropbox, Gmail, Google, Netflix, and YouTube — all websites. You also find apps that connect to stores for NOOK, Google, and Samsung.

Looking from the NOOK

You need an active Wi-Fi signal to use the Internet from your tablet. Without it, your browser will load, but won't browse.

Going onto the Internet from the Tab 4 NOOK is very much like making the same journey from a desktop or laptop computer, except that you'll be using your fingers to do the walking and the screen is smaller. See Figure 8-1.

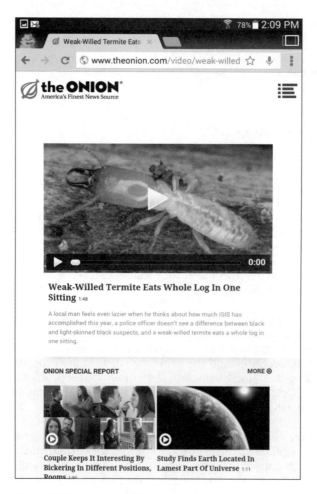

Figure 8-1: A page in the Chrome browser. Don't confuse satirical *The Onion* with other websites reporting actual news.

Omnibox on your tablet

One of Chrome's claims to fame is what Google calls the Omnibox, the merging of the address bar and search bar. If you typed in some or all of a recognized website, Chrome would suggest the full address based on your prior history or from its own vast records of other searches. On the other hand, if you were to enter the words or phrases of a search, Chrome assumes you want to use a search engine and it'll bring you to the most obvious of all suspects: Google.com.

Keep these things in mind while browsing:

- ✔ If you know the name of the web page you want to go to, just tap the address bar near the top of the page. Then use the onscreen virtual keyboard to enter its name.

- ✔ You don't need to enter *http://.* Most times you don't have to enter *www,* either.

- ✔ When you finish typing a web address, tap the Return key at the lower-right corner of the keyboard.

- ✔ If the browser correctly predicts what you want to enter, just tap the web address. See Figure 8-2.

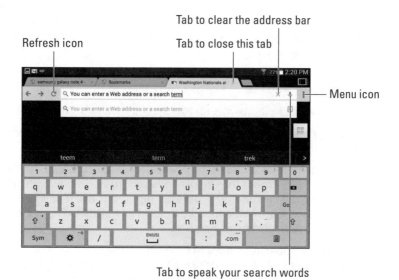

Tab to clear the address bar

Tab to close this tab

Refresh icon

Menu icon

Tab to speak your search words

Figure 8-2: Modern browsers like Chrome merge the address bar and search bar.

- If you swipe a web page up toward the top of the device, the address bar and tabs disappear. To see the address bar again, swipe down.

The Chrome browser has a few more particulars:

- To refresh or reload a web page, tap the curved arrow icon to the left of the address bar.
- To stop a web page from loading — a valuable tool if there's a hangup — tap the X symbol in the address bar. It's to the left when a page is coming up; when the page comes up, that X is replaced by the refresh icon.
- Anything a mouse can do on a computer, you do with a tap of your finger. "Click" a link by tapping the highlighted text (often marked in blue). Select an item or make a choice from a list by tapping an icon, picture, or word.
- If the web page is too small for you to easily jab at with your finger, zoom in: Place two fingers on the page and spread them apart. This works on most but not all pages.

I'm going to make a reasonable assumption that most people have an understanding of the basic operations of a browser. I want to point out Chrome's advanced, less obvious features.

Start by examining the browser's menu. Get there by tapping the Menu icon (pointed out in Figure 8-3) in the upper-right corner of any page in Chrome.

Here are some of the choices:

- **New Tab.** You can open many tabs at once, flitting from website to website. Although after about three tabs, the real screen gets too crowded to easily use. You can also open a new tab by tapping the blank tab above the address bar.
- **New Incognito Tab.** This new tab section has a bit more privacy than a standard web visit. I explain more later in this chapter.
- **Bookmarks.** Tap to see favorite pages you've noted.
- **Recent Tabs.** You can revisit web pages on tabs you recently closed. This is generally a good thing for busy users.

    Chrome makes it easy to see websites you've visited. Me? I've got nothing to hide except for the obvious record of time-wasting distractions that eat away from my ordinarily highly productive writing sessions. Use the Privacy option, which I discuss later in this chapter, to clear the Recent tabs and browsing history.

- **History.** You can go back in time within the same session, or days past. And if you have other devices using the same Google account, you can see their history. The History panel can hold dozens of entries. You can clear your browsing data by tapping the button at the bottom of the History screen, or clear away individual visits by tapping the X beside a particular entry.

✔ **Share.** Tell the world, or at least your friends, family, and coworkers about pages you've found. I discuss sharing later in this chapter.

✔ **Print.** Tap here to print from your Tab 4 NOOK to most local printers with Wi-Fi or Bluetooth communication facilities; you will have to set up this communication link beforehand.

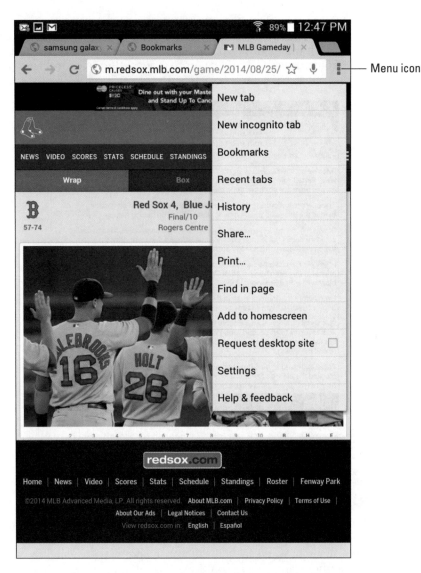

— Menu icon

Figure 8-3: Tap the Menu icon in the upper-right corner of the Chrome browser to display a set of powerful options.

✔ **Find in Page.** Search for a word, name, or phrase within the current web page. As you type, results get more specific. You can't search for an image, only words in the text. See Figure 8-4.

✔ **Add to Homescreen.** You can create a shortcut to a web page, a very useful hyper-bookmark. I discuss this later in this chapter, in the section about bookmarks.

✔ **Request Desktop Site.** Websites want to show you their special, reduced *mobile* versions. Which you may not like. To ask that sites treat your tablet as if it were a desktop, tap to place a check mark in Request Desktop Site. You might have to reload or re-request the page for this to take effect.

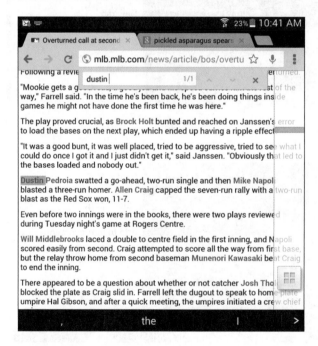

Figure 8-4: Find in Page lets you search for words anywhere in the text of a website.

Speaking Your Mind with Voice Search

But hear now, here's something you can't always do on a desktop computer: Tap the microphone icon (at the right side of the address bar) and dictate your desires. You'll see a little box on screen with a slightly larger icon of a microphone and the instructions, "Speak now."

That's your cue. Speak now, as clearly as you can, in the direction of the tiny microphone on your tablet. I find the accuracy of the voice recognition to be quite good, understanding nearly all of my search requests about 85 percent of the time.

Voice Search can help with simple questions like these:

- What time is it in Tblisi?
- Will it rain tomorrow in Casablanca?
- Where was Alexander Graham Bell born?
- How do you say "That's enough" in Latin?

The system's smart enough to make some logical leaps. I asked, "Will I need an umbrella today?" and it figured I wanted the forecast.

The d**ned thing can even understand many curse words, at least to the point of ignoring them if they're an unnecessary part of a question. See Figure 8-5.

Using a Search Engine Other Than Chrome

Google has become so popular it is almost a generic term. Though Google Inc. has a squad of lawyers prepared to do battle in defense of their trademark, you'll still hear people saying they intend to "google Teddy Roosevelt" when what they mean to say is they intend to "use the Google.com search engine to find out more about President Theodore Roosevelt."

You don't have to stick with Google. Here's how to change the default search engine:

1. **Tap the Chrome icon on the Home screen.**
2. **Tap the Menu icon in the upper-right corner.**
3. **Tap Settings.**
4. **In the Basics section, tap Search Engine.**
5. **Choose an alternative.**

You don't have to change search engines if you just want to try another one from time to time. Just go to Chrome, and in the address bar, type the site: yahoo.com, bing.com, ask.com, and aol.com.

Figure 8-5: Voice Search does a pretty good job of interpreting your spoken commands.

Skipping the Browser to Search the Web

If you need an expressway to look something up, there's a direct exit from the Home screen through the Google app. Tap the blue lowercase g icon pointed out in Figure 8-6.

You can use the onscreen keyboard to enter a standard search; then tap the magnifying glass icon.

The Google app also has voice recognition; you can talk to the tablet. Say, "Okay, Google" and wait for a pleasant beep in response; the microphone icon at the right side of the search bar turns red. Speak clearly and evenly to the tablet.

You're offered the option of using Chrome, or Samsung's adaptation of Chrome, which is cleverly called *Internet.* (I suggest sticking with Chrome for consistency.)

Tap here to see a search panel

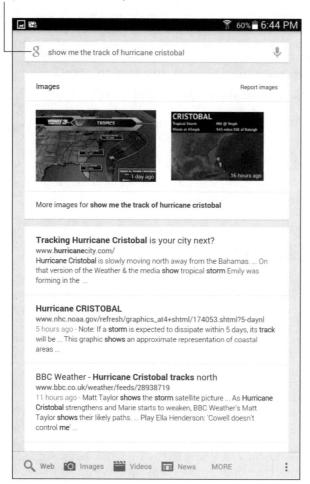

Figure 8-6: The Google app gives you just the search functions of a browser.

Sharing Is Caring

With apologies to Lennon and McCartney of the Beatles: "I read the news today, oh boy, and saw a photograph that blew my mind." It was a picture of a line of about 20 people waiting at a bus stop. Each and every person was staring intently into his own tablet or a smartphone, lost in his own world. Presumably, the oncoming bus driver was paying attention.

Anyhow, my point: Though sometimes it is hard to believe it, the act of browsing the web can (and should) be a communal activity. I know that I love to find funny or interesting stories or entire pages that I can send to my wife, my kids, my friends, and total strangers.

Although you *could* copy a web page and paste it into an email, that's time-consuming (and doesn't guarantee that this pearl can be viewed properly). The better way is to send a *link* for the page you want to share. Here's how:

1. **In Chrome, open the web page you want to share.**

2. **Tap the Menu icon in the upper-right corner.**

3. **Tap Share.**

   A menu opens, as shown in Figure 8-7.

4. **Pick a way to send the page.**

   The Share Via menu offers just about every possible means of communication from your Tab 4 NOOK.

Signing in to Chrome

An advantage of using the Chrome browser is its ability to sync between all of the devices you attach to the same account: desktops, laptops, tablets, smartphones included. It won't work with chrome bumpers on a 1935 SJ LaGrande Dual-Cowl Duesenberg Phaeton, but if you can afford to keep one of those in your garage, you can also afford to hire a personal assistant to record all your bookmarks and preferences in a leather-bound journal.

Here's what happens when you sign in to the Chrome browser while using an active Wi-Fi connection: All of your web page bookmarks, tabs, history, and other browser preferences are saved to your Google account. At the same time, any changes you made while using another computer, tablet, or smartphone that uses the same Google account are synced to your Tab 4 NOOK. You can manage the data by going to the Google Dashboard. Signing into Chrome also opens the door to personalizations you may have made to other Google services such as Gmail, YouTube, and Google Maps.

If you've set up your Tab 4 NOOK to automatically sign in to your Google account each time you turn it on, you're all set.

To turn on or off automatic sign-in, do this:

1. **From the Home screen, tap the Chrome icon.**

2. **Tap the Menu icon in the upper-right corner.**

3. **Tap Settings.**

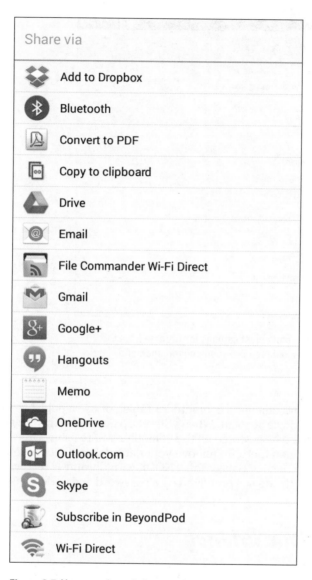

Figure 8-7: You can share links to web pages at the tap of a few onscreen buttons.

4. **From the Basics section, tap the Google sign-in name you registered when you set up your Tab 4 NOOK.**

   See Figure 8-8.

5. **Tap to remove or enter a check mark in the Auto Sign-In option.**

   And no, that isn't my email address.

Figure 8-8: You can adjust settings for Chrome from this page, striking a balance between convenience and possible privacy loss.

If you borrow someone's computer or tablet, or use a public computer, don't sign in to your Google account. When you set up Chrome with your Google account, a copy of your data is stored on the computer you're using. Other users can get that information there. To remove your data, delete the user you're signed in as. Using your Samsung Galaxy Tab 4 NOOK with Chrome is relatively safe, as long as you keep the device protected by a password and under your control.

Protecting Your Privacy

You can go back to the future or ahead to the past by tapping the ← (back) arrow or → (forward) arrow at the far left of the address bar. The back arrow is available when you've gone at least one page forward by tapping a link. The forward arrow is usable any time you've gone back at least one page in the current tab.

Being a revisionist: Clearing your history

You can also consult your history of web browsing; see Figure 8-9. You can clear the History list on your Tab 4 NOOK quite easily. Here's how:

1. Tap the Menu icon within the Chrome browser.

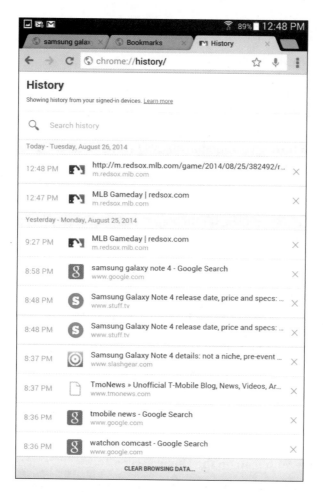

Figure 8-9: Your browser keeps track of where you've been; it even records the date and time.

2. **Tap History.**

   Other options:

   - *Recent Tabs.* If you're signed in to Chrome, you can see web pages that have been opened on your Tab 4 NOOK as well as any desktop, laptop, smartphone, or other tablet that shares the account.

   - *Most Visited.* If you select Recent Tabs you will see another option now displayed at the bottom of the screen. Tap Most Visited to be offered a page full of just that: the most often-visited Web page on your tablet.

When your history is displayed, look for the little option bar at the bottom of the page, below all of that information you don't want recorded.

3. Tap Clear Browsing Data.

Don't assume that any search, web page visit, email, message, chat, or any other action you perform on the Internet is private.

To begin with, your *Internet Service Provider (ISP)* probably records all traffic that goes through its equipment. And then the web page at the end of the line will likely keep track of any user that visits — or at least their IP address, which is the electronic connection between your Wi-Fi modem or wired modem and the Internet.

If you use a different browser on your Galaxy Tab 4 NOOK, check the settings page to find a Security and Privacy panel. You can sweep away *local* evidence of your excursions on the Internet.

Delving deeper into privacy settings

Internet users can never expect to have complete and total privacy; even if you keep your own tablet clear, your requests to search engines and Internet providers are all routinely recorded or logged or otherwise noted.

You can do some things to protect your privacy on your own device, though. Google's Chrome (and other browsers) lets you wipe away local traces of your Internet travels.

Here's how to clean up within Chrome:

1. Tap the Web icon on the Home screen.

Or, tap the Chrome icon in the Apps menu or any shortcut you may have created for Chrome.

2. Tap the Menu icon in the upper-right corner.

3. Tap Settings.

4. In the Advanced section, tap Privacy.

5. Tap Clear Browsing Data at the upper right.

A menu opens, as shown in Figure 8-10.

6. Tap a check mark in the privacy options you want to turn on:

- **Clear Browsing History.** Erases the web addresses of all pages you've visited.

- **Clear the Cache.** The *cache* stored of web pages you've visited or addresses you've entered.

Figure 8-10: Clear Browsing Data options swipe most footprints, but your ISP and various websites may still remember you fondly.

- **Clear Cookies, Site Data.** Many websites, especially those hoping to sell you something, leave behind a small file known as a *cookie*. The cookie might indicate, "This user has been here before and visited the following pages within this site." Or the cookie might say, "This visitor is a registered user and is granted full access."

- **Clear Saved Passwords.** You can let Chrome track passwords you use for certain websites; you'll see an onscreen message from the browser asking if you want that done. Add a check mark here to erase them from memory.

- **Clear Autofill Data.** The browser can track certain common fields for online forms: your name and address, for example. Tap a check mark here to clear the answers.

7. **Tap Clear to zap the information.**

Close any currently open websites in Chrome that you don't want visible after you delete your history and cache.

Adjusting content settings

Chrome allows you to make adjustments to content settings. See Figure 8-11. To get to the page where you can adjust these settings, do this:

1. **Tap the Web icon on the Home screen.**

   Or tap the Chrome icon within the Apps menu or any shortcut you may have created for Chrome.

2. **Tap the Menu icon in the upper-right corner.**

3. **Tap Settings.**

4. **In the Advanced section, tap Content Settings.**

The following sections talk about the options in this menu.

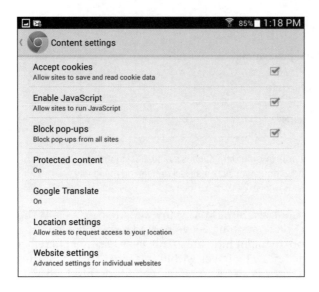

Figure 8-11: Content settings let you kill cookies on contact.

Accepting or declining cookies

I mention cookies a bit earlier, which some websites leave behind on your system. Some may be perfectly benign, like a reminder of the last page you visited on a complex site. Others may be not so innocent, like an attempt by an advertiser or other entity to track your movement around the web.

In theory, the cookies are anonymous. Your tablet is just a number to the cookie-dropper. However, if the cookie comes from a site that requires you to sign in, well then you're not all that anonymous after all.

You can tell Chrome (and most other browsers) that you don't want to allow cookies. The bad news is that *some* websites won't allow you to get very deep into their content without being able to leave cookies behind.

It's your decision. I allow cookies, but also regularly (usually daily, sometimes more frequently) clear them away. Sometimes I tell the browser not to accept cookies and wait to see which websites object; if they do, I consider whether this site has a legitimate reason to put a note within my tablet or computer.

Enabling or disabling JavaScript

JavaScript is a programming language that animates or customizes web pages. You can remove the check mark from the Enable JavaScript setting if you'd like. You may find that some websites will not run properly, or you may never notice the difference.

In the past JavaScript has been accused of causing problems on its own, or allowing itself to be hijacked by evildoers seeking to implant viruses or steal information or otherwise foul the swimming pool. That is less common today, and in any case a tablet running Android is, to some extent, less vulnerable to this sort of attack than is a desktop or laptop computer.

Block pop-ups

Among the many annoyances used by advertisers . . . to make a buck off of us innocent Internet users is a *pop-up ad.* It might appear in front of a news article that you want to read, or block an entertainment page.

Once again, there's a potential downside: Some websites may not run right if you block pop-ups, and some pop-ups blast right through this protection anyway.

I generally leave pop-up blocking on, and hope for the best.

Protected content

This is generally a benign setting, and may not apply to all users. When you allow Chrome to use the Protected content setting, the site authenticates your device to confirm that it's allowed to display certain content like music or videos. These providers place a special type of cookie, called a device credential, on your tablet or computer.

Location settings

If you're going to allow yourself to become impressed by your tablet's ability to help you find the nearest gas station or helium balloon-refilling station, you're going to have to allow the browser to provide information to sites about where you are.

Your tablet has a GPS which can pinpoint your location to a few tens of yards in proper conditions; in addition to that, search engines are usually able to figure out your approximate location based on where your Wi-Fi router connects to the Internet.

Is this an invasion of your privacy? It probably is, but there's not much you can do to avoid it except to not use a tablet or a smartphone or a telephone; I think the more important thing to concentrate on is working to limit the amount of other information you divulge to outsiders.

Other content settings

You can turn off Google Translate, which decodes foreign language websites for you, and also examine website settings, which are yet another form of cookies. If you see a site here that you don't expect to revisit or don't want visiting you, tap its name and then tap Clear Stored Data.

Going incognito in Chrome

One way to reduce your exposure to prying eyes is to open an *incognito window* within Chrome. The browser automatically declines to save a record of whatever page you've opened or downloaded within that window. See Figure 8-12.

Specifically, your browsing history including pages you open and files downloaded while in incognito mode aren't recorded in your browsing and download histories. Any new cookies installed in your tablet while incognito are deleted *after you close all incognito windows.*

You can switch between incognito and regular mode browsing, and even have both types of windows open at the same time. But the extra protection is only available in the incognito session or sessions.

Chrome will quite subtly mark the fact that a window is *incognito* (Latin for "unknown") by placing a tiny icon of a spy, complete with dark glasses, at the left side of the screen.

The incognito icon

Figure 8-12: Going incognito removes most traces of web browsing from your device. Notice the little spy guy in the upper left?

You can open an incognito window two ways:

- ✓ Press and hold (or long-press) a link on a web page. A small panel opens; choose Open in Incognito Tab.
- ✓ From Chrome, tap the Menu icon and then tap New Incognito Tab.

To exit an incognito window, click the X at the corner of the tab.

Customizing Chrome Sync settings

Although most users want to synchronize everything that uses their Google account, you can turn off specific utilities. Here's how:

1. **Tap the Web icon on the Home screen.**

   Or, tap the Chrome icon in the Apps menu or any shortcut you may have created for Chrome.

2. **Tap the Menu icon in the upper-right corner.**

3. **Tap Settings.**

4. **Tap the Basic panel on the left side, if it isn't already selected.**

5. **Tap your account name.**

6. **Under Services, tap the Sync option.**

   You see a panel of data types. If you put a check mark under Sync Everything, then everything is synced.

7. **If you remove the check mark from Sync Everything, choose from the settings: Autofill, Bookmarks, History, Passwords, and Open.**

   Back out of Chrome by pressing the Back key, or return to the Home screen.

Encrypting your Google account data

Google promises that all synced data is *encrypted* (coded) when it travels between your computer and Google's servers. You can apply an extra level of encryption to the data stored on your own device. To become the encryption keeper on your tablet, do this:

1. **Tap the Web icon on the Home screen.**

   Or, tap the Chrome icon in the Apps menu or any shortcut you may have created for Chrome.

2. **Tap the Menu icon in the upper right corner of the Chrome page.**

3. **Tap Settings.**

4. **Tap the Basic panel on the left side of the screen if it is not already selected.**

5. **Tap your account name.**

6. **Under Services, tap the Sync option.**

   You'll see a panel of Data Types.

7. **Tap Encryption.**

   A panel opens.

8. **Tap the open circle next to Encrypt all with passphrase.**

9. **Enter a passphrase of a few words.**

10. **Retype the passphrase when you're asked to confirm.**

The passphrase doesn't go to Google, and you're responsible for keeping it in mind. If you forget the passphrase, you have to reset the sync process within your Google account.

Turning on bandwidth management

Chrome users can retrieve most web pages through Google's servers instead of directly from wherever they are stored. Although it ordinarily adds at least one extra hop — and a bit of time — between your request and the moment a web page appears on the screen of your tablet, Google offers the possibility of more than making up for the lost time by *compressing* the web page so that it moves faster to you. This *bandwidth management* scheme works by converting certain types of images to smaller files; on average, about 60 percent of web pages consist of images. In addition, the Google technology also performs other tricks to reduce the overall size of web pages.

You can try bandwidth management and see if it works well for you. If it causes problems, turn it off. Here's how to turn it on:

1. **Tap the Web icon on the Home screen.**

Or, tap the Chrome icon within the Apps menu or any shortcut you may have created for Chrome.

2. **Tap the Menu icon in the upper-right corner of the Chrome page.**

3. **Tap Settings.**

4. **Tap the Advanced panel on the left side of the screen if it is not already selected.**

5. **Tap Bandwidth Management in the panel on the right.**

6. **Tap Reduce Data Usage.**

7. **On the Data Savings page, make sure that the switch at the upper right is On.**

If not, tap and slide it to the On position.

You can see a report that estimates the amount of compression that has been applied in the last month. If the report says 25%, in rough terms that means that pages that've been compressed through the Google servers have been on average about 25 percent smaller by the time they arrived on your tablet, and your system has responded about 25 percent faster than it would have without this feature enabled.

Preloading web pages

Preloading pages is another bandwidth management feature. This is part of a technology called *predictive computing*.

If you turn on this feature, the browser examines the current page and tries to predict one or more pages you're likely to request.

For example, if you're looking at an online retailer and reading the description of a new camera, the browser might note that there are two big buttons nearby that read, Specifications and More Pictures. Chrome might *preload* one or both pages into the tablet's memory. If it guessed correctly, you might save a few seconds of your invaluable time.

On the version of Chrome offered for the Wi-Fi–only Samsung Galaxy Tab 4 NOOK, just turn on Preload Webpages by putting a check mark in the box, or vice versa.

Most users will find both preloading and bandwidth management to be worthwhile. However, if your tablet slows down or certain pages don't display properly or at all, try turning off Preload Webpages or Bandwidth Management (or both) to see if that solves the problem.

Leaving Bread Crumbs: Bookmarking

Sometimes you very much want to leave behind traces of places you have been on the web. You can insert *bookmarks* that record web addresses for pages you expect to want to visit again.

Among the nice things about browser bookmarks is that they don't fall out when you turn your NOOK upside down. See a bookmark in progress in Figure 8-13. Here's how to create a bookmark for a page:

1. **From Chrome, visit the web page you want to bookmark.**

2. **Tap the Bookmark (star) icon in the upper-right corner of the address bar.**

   An unassigned web page has an empty or open star; when it's book-marked, the star is filled in black.

3. **Edit or skip to Step 4:**

   - *Name.* Chrome offers a suggestion, but you can tap in the field and change the name.

   - *URL.* This is the web address for the page you are bookmarking (in geekspeak, its uniform resource locator). Leave it as is.

   - *Folder.* You can store your bookmarks in one of the predefined folders or create your own folder.

   I create folders by type: Travel, Banking, Shopping, and the like. You can scroll through the list of bookmarks with judicious finger swipes.

4. **Tap Save.**

If you don't create a bookmark while viewing a web page, you can go back in time to the Most Visited tab. Open the web page and tap the Bookmark icon.

Figure 8-13: You can add a favorite or important page.

Editing or deleting a bookmark

To change a bookmark's name or folder, or to delete a bookmark, do this:

1. **Go to the folder holding the bookmark.**

2. **Press and hold the bookmark. See Figure 8-14.**

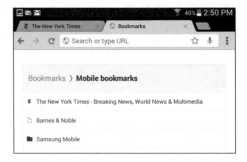

Figure 8-14: Visit Bookmarks to return to a page or to edit the list.

3. **Choose an option.**

   You can open the website in a new tab, open it in an incognito tab, or edit or delete the bookmark.

Adding a web page to your Home screen

The ultimate bookmark adds a shortcut to a web address on your Home screen. You can even create a folder of favorite sites and gather them there.

Here's how to add a shortcut to a web page on your Home screen:

1. **From Chrome, visit the web page you want to bookmark.**

2. **Tap the Menu icon in the upper-right corner.**

3. **Tap Add to Homescreen.**

   The system automatically adds the website name . You can edit the name if you want; the address won't change. See Figure 8-15.

4. **Tap Add.**

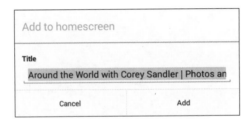

Figure 8-15: Putting a shortcut on the Home screen lets you visit pages without even starting the browser.

Popping open multiple browser tabs

The long-gone but not forgotten by some comedy troupe *Firesign Theater* once based an entire evening's performance around the essential question, "How can you be in two places at once, when you're not anywhere at all?" On Google Chrome, while you sit wherever you may think you are, and be in many more places at once.

You can open multiple *tabs* within one browsing session. Unused extra tabs lurk behind open screens; just tap an empty tab to visit other sites or conduct searches without closing earlier tabs. See Figure 8-16. Move to another by tapping any tab title. To close a tab, tap the X in its right corner. You can touch and move a tab's order onscreen.

The other way to open a new tab is to press and hold (or long-press) a link you see on a web page. When you do that, you get these options:

✔ **Open in New Tab.** Select this one to do just what it offers, automatically opening a tab based on the link you chose.

✔ **Open in Incognito Tab.** This opens a new tab based on the link, but makes it incognito. Its details are in this chapter's "Going incognito in Chrome."

Another tab is open here   Tap to open a new tab

Figure 8-16: Multiple tabs are a great way to keep important pages close at all times.

Part III
Reading Electronics

Visit www.dummies.com/extras/samnsunggalaxytab4nook for help setting up separate accounts on the Tab 4.

In this part . . .

- Figure out how to buy something from the NOOK Shop.
- Categorize books, magazines, and newspaper in your NOOK library.
- Read on your NOOK.
- Find other sources for eBooks.

9

Looking into the NOOK Library

*I*n the end, it doesn't matter what medium you use to get your message across. The technology is merely the means of transport for ideas. The Samsung Galaxy Tab 4 NOOK is merely another way to read the printed word and absorb its content into our souls.

This chapter looks at the Tab 4 NOOK as a reading tablet, and specifically as an extension of the NOOK Shop operated by Barnes & Noble. Chapter 10 explores other sources of reading material and multimedia for your Tab 4 NOOK.

Rooting Around in Your NOOK Store

I'm going way out on a limb here and guess that the reason you purchased the NOOK version of the Samsung tablet is that you actually intend to do some reading: books, magazines, newspapers, and catalogs. Good news! That's just about as easy as tapping your finger.

And don't worry about running out of space for books. Your NOOK account comes with unlimited use of an online archive from which you can get titles anytime you have a Wi-Fi connection.

Your Samsung Galaxy Tab 4 NOOK comes with a few free books, plus samples of others. So you could, if you want, jump right in and start reading. I explain how to turn the pages and personalize the experience later in this chapter. But first, you might want to go shopping.

And you get a regular set of personalized recommendations. The more you buy, the more appropriate the suggestions become. See Figure 9-1.

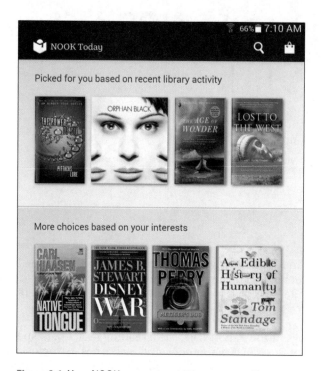

Figure 9-1: Your NOOK suggests additions to your library.

The NOOK Shop on the Galaxy Tab 4 NOOK can only be portrait mode (taller than wide). You can scroll up on the page to see special offerings in each of the departments. See Figure 9-2.

Here's how to get to the NOOK Shop:

1. **From the Home screen, tap the NOOK Shop app.**

   Or, tap one of the advertising banners that promote the bestseller list or special sales.

2. **If you wind up somewhere *other* than the main shop, tap the shopping bag icon in the upper left.**

   Just like when you walk into a brick-and-mortar bookstore, you have to make your way past promotions for new titles and specials. What you see today is likely to be different from what you saw yesterday or will find tomorrow.

3. **Tap a department.**

   The departments — Books, Magazines (includes Catalogs), Movies & TV, Kids, Apps, Newspapers, and Comics — are on the right side of the screen.

4. **Explore the categories or look for new releases or bestsellers.**

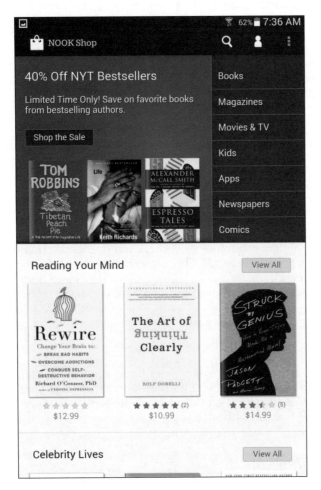

Figure 9-2: The front page of the NOOK Shop has sales, suggestions, and a set of shopping categories on the right.

Finding a specific book

As much as I love to browse the aisles (physical or electronic) of a good bookstore, sometimes I know exactly what I want.

The NOOK boob tube

The NOOK Shop offers lots of movies, TV shows, and specialty videos. You'll find free previews of some movies, and free episodes from TV series. You can't get HD playback (because of what B&N says are licensing restrictions); you'll see the SD (standard definition) version. It's not a big deal on a small screen; it is difficult if not impossible to tell the difference. However, if you buy an HD version of a video, you can watch it in high definition on other devices, including a computer and Roku players that attach to televisions.

You can buy videos, in which case you own them and can watch them over and over again;

if you have children, you'll understand that concept right away. Some videos are available as rentals, generally for about one-third to one-half the price of buying. When you rent a video, you have 30 days after download to start watching; once you start playing a movie or show, you have 24 hours to finish.

The Tab 4 NOOK supports UltraViolet, which lets you stream or download a video to multiple compatible devices. For releases in that format, sign up for yet another account, this one with UltraViolet.

To search for a particular book or periodical, tap the Search (magnifying glass) icon at the top of the NOOK Shop screen. Use the keyboard to type your entry. My search results are in Figure 9-3. Or, press and hold the icon to the left of the spacebar of the onscreen keyboard and tap a method:

- Use voice recognition to say what you're looking for.
- Handwrite your entry on the touchpad.

Scroll through the results by dragging your finger up or down. A blue banner shows the prices on the B&N site. If you see a gray Purchased label, you already bought that title for the current account; once you pay, you can always download it again without paying again.

Buying a book

Sooner or later you're going to find a book you want to add to your library. On behalf of authors and publishers everywhere, we thank you for your investment in fine literature of all kind. Here's what's next:

1. **Tap the cover to see its details.**

   Sometimes you're offered a sample from the book. To drop a not-very-subtle hint to someone about the perfect birthday gift for you, tap the Share icon (see Figure 9-4) to send an email detailing what you've found. You can also rate and review your thoughts about the title, posting to Facebook or Twitter.

Figure 9-3: Search for eBooks by author, title, or subject. Tap one to learn more about it, or to buy.

2. **To buy an eBook, tap the blue box that shows the price.**

   Are you sure? You're asked to confirm your purchase.

3. **Confirm your purchase.**

   Some books are offered for the can't-beat-it price of free. Publishers do this to try and build an audience for a series of books. If you ask for a copy of a free book, you're still asked to confirm your decision.

   The eBook is charged to your credit card and the title comes to your Tab 4 NOOK, usually within a few seconds. If an eBook's download is interrupted because of a problem with the wireless connection or other causes, the download automatically resumes the next time it gets a chance.

Share icon

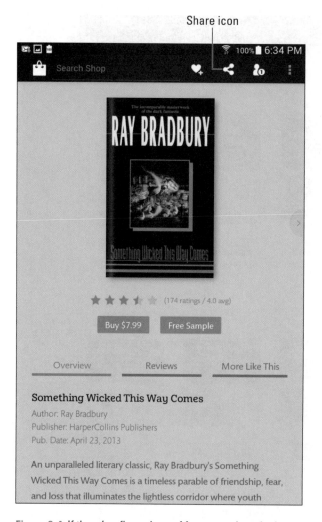

Figure 9-4: If there's a finer piece of fantasy written in the English language than Ray Bradbury's *Something Wicked This Way Comes,* I've not found it.

The new item appears on the Active shelf on the Home screen and in your library. And it wears a New badge until you open it.

Buying magazines or newspapers

You can buy individual issues of a newspaper or magazine, or subscribe to daily, weekly, or monthly delivery. Just as in the world of paper and ink, the best deals come with longer-term subscriptions. Once you buy, the first issue downloads immediately.

Nearly every magazine and newspaper offers free 14-day trials; you can get one free trial for each publication. If you cancel the subscription before the end of the trial, your credit card isn't charged. Otherwise, deliveries continue and your credit card is charged automatically at the monthly subscription rate. To cancel a periodical subscription, go to your account at www.nook.com, log in, and go to the Manage Subscriptions section.

To buy a single issue or to subscribe, follow these steps:

1. **Tap the cover.**

   You'll see the price for the current issue, and elsewhere on the page you can see the price for a monthly subscription. See Figure 9-5.

Figure 9-5: Getting a free trial allows you 14 days to decide, and the rate is usually better than buying individual issues.

2. **To buy the latest issue only, tap Buy Current Issue. To buy a subscription, tap Free Trial.**

   If you subscribe, you get the first issue and have 14 days to decide whether to continue. If you cancel within those 14 days, you'll have received that first issue for free. If you *don't* cancel, you're on the hook for at least one month at the subscription price — but you can cancel any time after then.

   It's almost a no-brainer: Take the free trial for any magazine or newspaper you want to try. The month-to-month subscription usually represents a significant savings over buying a single issue, and you can cancel any time. Note that you can only take a free trial once for any particular publication.

3. **Tap Confirm.**

   The issue downloads.

4. **Tap the Read button.**

Subscribing to catalogs

Catalogs are free; the companies that provide them very much want you salivating over their shoes, dresses, fruitcakes, and gadgets. Some of the first offerings are from major sellers like L.L. Bean, Sharper Image, Omaha Steaks, Pottery Barn, and Ross-Simons. See Figure 9-6.

When you tap the cover of a catalog, you wind up on a purchase screen very much like one for a magazine. You'll see two choices, and both are free:

- **Current Edition:** Just this once.
- **Free Subscription:** You're going to get each new edition of the catalog.

Many include links that let you jump to an order page on the company's website. Some catalogs have links to video demonstrations and other bells and whistles.

Paying the bill

Unless you say otherwise, your credit card is charged when you buy something from Barnes & Noble. It's all done for you; there are no receipts to sign.

If you have a Barnes & Noble gift card, you can add its value to your account.

1. **Tap the Menu icon in the upper-right corner.**

2. **Tap Shop Settings.**

3. **Edit your credit card or gift card listings.**

   If you have any problems with a gift card or credit card, call customer service at the NOOK Shop or use its chat line.

Figure 9-6: Catalogs offer beautiful color images and enticing descriptions of all sorts of products you never knew you needed.

Archiving to the NOOK cloud

Have you ever been accused of walking around with your head in a cloud? So have I. And so, too, does your Tab 4 NOOK. Every registered user is automatically set up with unlimited storage back at the Barnes & Noble mothership (also known as *the cloud*).

When you archive, the file is removed from your NOOK, leaving behind only an icon or picture of its cover to remind you; any time you want to get that reading material, you can *restore* it from the NOOK cloud. See Figure 9-7.

Figure 9-7: You can fill the NOOK archive with as much B&N electronic material as you want; grab it with a tap. You can see I've archived two (2) items.

Why might you archive something?

- You want to clear some space in the built-in memory or microSD card.

- Your Tab 4 NOOK or other NOOK device is stolen or permanently deceased; sign in to the same account to restore all the files to a new device or app.

You can archive any of these from the NOOK cloud: books, magazines, newspapers, or catalogs. You can also reinstall apps or videos you have purchased.

 The NOOK cloud can't store personal files that you move from a computer using a USB cable, from an email attachment, or by downloading from an Internet website other than the NOOK Shop. However, you can connect your NOOK to a computer and make a backup folder of your personal material there.

Archiving an item to the NOOK cloud

 The original version of the online instruction manual for the Tab 4 NOOK somehow managed to leave this out completely; I expect B&N will eventually update their publication but here's the secret:

1. **Go to the NOOK library.**

2. **Press and hold on the book cover *at the same time* you press the + side of the Volume key (on the right side of the tablet).**

3. Choose Archive. See Figure 9-8.

The book or other publication goes away, but if you tap the Menu icon in the upper-right corner of the library, you see View Archive. From there, you can restore items. (You must have an active Wi-Fi signal to archive or restore, of course.)

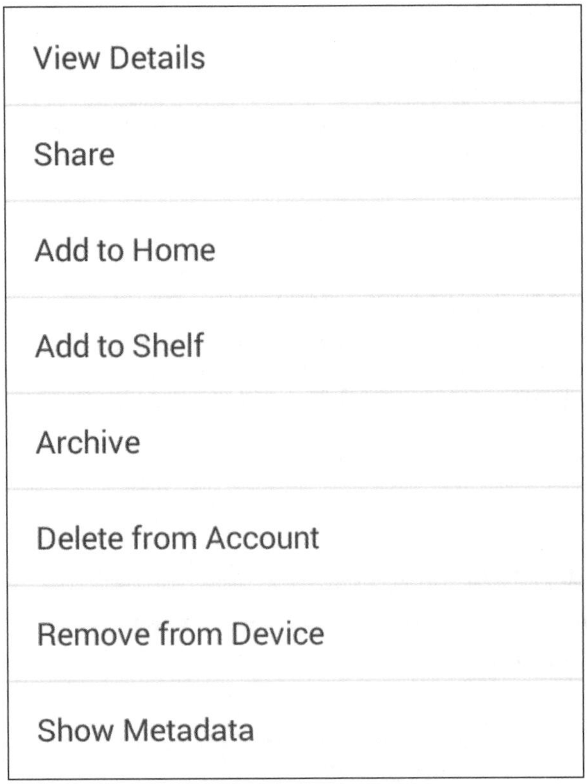

View Details
Share
Add to Home
Add to Shelf
Archive
Delete from Account
Remove from Device
Show Metadata

Figure 9-8: Archiving something that you got from the NOOK Store places it in storage in the cloud, freeing up tablet space.

There's another way, with a bit of confusing terminology:

1. Go to the NOOK library.

2. Press and hold on the cover of the book.

3. Tap Remove from Device.

Yes, I know this sounds like the book will be deleted and gone forever, but that's not correct. It's removed from the hardware and kept in your archive even though it doesn't say that exactly. You can get it back by going to the archive; just tap the Menu icon in your NOOK library.

There's a big difference between *archiving* and *deleting*. If you *archive* an item, you can get it back from the NOOK cloud. If you *delete* any item, you erase it from your NOOK and can't get it without going back to the original source.

After you buy a book from Barnes & Noble, you own the license to that title on up to six devices or apps registered to your account. You can leave the book file on your Tab 4 NOOK or you can archive it back to your account, which removes it from the tablet but keeps it in your available material in the NOOK cloud. The key: All devices or applications must be registered to the same account.

Performing a sync or refresh

You can also *sync* your Tab 4 NOOK to your NOOK account; doing so keeps it updated with all your currently purchased content. Syncing also lets you know about tablet updates, book loan offers, and other notices.

Items you've archived aren't synced.

Follow these steps:

1. **Go to the NOOK library.**
2. **Tap the Menu icon in the upper-right corner.**
3. **Tap Refresh.**

B&N goodies

What happens if you take your NOOK to an actual Barnes & Noble store, where there are walls and floors and ceilings? The device asks if you'd like to connect to the in-store network. (Tap Connect to agree; tap Dismiss to disagree.) If you connect, you can get:

✓ A free pass to read or sample certain NOOK eBooks for one hour per day. You can read as many books as you want while you're in the store, although the 60-minute limit applies for each title.

✓ Exclusive content and offers available only to NOOK owners using the in-store network.

Can I Borrow That?

With the Tab 4 NOOK, a lender and a borrower you can be. You can invite friends from your Contacts list, from Facebook or Google, or by email. See Figure 9-9.

There are just a few catches:

- ✔ You can loan only books that have a LendMe badge.
- ✔ You can loan a book only once, and only for 14 days. After then it comes back to your library.
- ✔ You can't read the book while you're loaning it to someone. (It's like a printed book in that way: It can't be in two places at once.)

Figure 9-9: Some books can be loaned (once) to friends or acquaintances with their own NOOK account.

Here's how to loan a book that has a LendMe badge:

1. **Press and hold on its cover.**

2. **Tap Share.**

3. **Tap LendMe.**

4. **Enter an email or select from your contacts, Facebook, or Twitter friends.**

   You can also write a short message, like: "Read this and let me know if it changes your entire political and philosophical view on life. If not, we'll never speak again." Or you can say something else.

You also can loan a book by lending the actual Tab 4 NOOK device to a trusted friend or acquaintance. If you do this, be aware that the person will have access to the Barnes & Noble store under your account name (but can't buy anything if your account requires a password to do so).

Here are a few more bits of legalese:

- ✔ You can lend only to users who have other registered B&N devices, or apps that run on other devices such as desktop or laptop computers, smartphones, and certain other tablets.

- ✔ You can send LendMe offers to any email address, but to accept, the recipient must have an email address associated with a Barnes & Noble online account. That means that person is a resident of the United States or Canada. An offer expires after seven days if it hasn't been accepted.

- ✔ You can't loan a book that's been loaned to you.

- ✔ You can't save a borrowed book to a microSD card or archive it to the NOOK cloud.

Being Your Own Librarian

The library is where all documents live on your NOOK, including books, periodicals, and personal files. The library is all inclusive, while the individual shelves for books, magazines, catalogs, and newspapers hold only files that the system recognizes as fitting that description.

Reading covers

To some extent, you actually can tell a book by its cover on the NOOK: not so much about what's inside, but a great deal about its status or stature in your collection.

- ✔ **New.** Freshly downloaded and ready to be opened. This badge goes away after the first time you open the document.

- ✔ **Sample.** A free sample of a book or other publication.

- ✔ **Download.** A publication that's either downloading or is waiting to be downloaded from the NOOK Shop.

- ✔ **Pre-order.** A title has been announced and is for sale, but isn't available for download yet. If you buy it, the book or publication will arrive at the first opportune moment and your credit card will be billed at that time.

- ✔ **Recommended.** A friend or contact has suggested that you check out this title.

- ✔ **LendMe.** A book that you can loan to someone.

- ✔ **Lent.** A book you're borrowing; the badge also indicates the number of days remaining on the loan. (While a book is loaned out, the original owner can't open it.)

Building your own shelves

When your NOOK arrives, it has basic shelves: Books, Magazines, Movies & TV, Kids, Catalogs, and Newspapers. Below that, My Shelves, is where you can create and fill your own collection in any way you choose. And finally, a section called My Files holds any personal files you have moved over to the Tab 4 NOOK.

Creating a shelf

You can create any shelf you want and call it anything you like. To create a shelf, do this:

1. **In My Library, tap the Menu icon in the upper right.**

2. **Tap Create New Shelf.**

3. **Use the keyboard to enter a name for the shelf.**

4. **Tap Save.**

Adding items to a shelf

Now you need to move things to your shelf:

1. **Press and hold on a book or a file in the list of items in your library.**

   A menu appears.

2. **Tap Add to Shelf.**

3. **Tap the name of a previously created shelf, or tap Add a New Shelf.**

   Rename a Shelf is an option. To get rid of a shelf, tap Remove a Shelf; tap OK to confirm.

In rare cases you may need to unlock a book or periodical that you bought through Barnes & Noble and that's protected using *Digital Rights Management (DRM)*. In that case enter your name, the email address associated with the B&N account, and the credit card number that you used to make the purchase.

Opening and Reading an eBook

You want to start reading. Naturally enough, you begin by opening a book. To do that, try either of these methods:

- Go to the Home screen and tap any cover you find in the NOOK library. See Figure 9-10.

- If you removed the NOOK app from the Home screen, tap the Apps icon in the lower right corner of the Home screen. Tap Apps and then tap NOOK Library. There you can tap any cover you find.

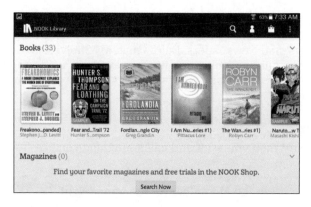

Figure 9-10: My library has 33 titles. Some were a gift from B&N (whether I wanted them or not), others I bought, and some were samples for research.

Turning the pages

Don't lick your finger and try to turn the page; that's unsanitary and will streak the glass. Instead, here's how to move within an eBook:

- **To turn to the next page, tap anywhere along the right edge of the page.**

- **To turn to the next page, swipe to the left.** Think of this as flicking a page from the right side of an opened book to flip it over. To go forward one page, place your finger on the right side of the page and keep it in contact as you slide it to the left.

- **To turn back to the previous page, tap anywhere along the left edge of the page.** Swipe to the right to go to previous pages. To swipe right, place your finger on the left side of the page and slide it to the right (flicking a page, in an electronic way).

- **Use one of the advanced tools.** What are they? Read on.

TIP

Page what?

You may see a page number on the screen. That page number probably won't correspond to the printed version of the book. And even between two Tab 4 NOOK tablets, page 47 on my screen might be page 52 on yours.

Here's the trick to comparing notes between eReaders, or between your tablet and a printed copy: Ask for a passage. Tap the Menu icon and choose Use the Find in Book.

Jumping to a page

With a printed book, you can flip through the pages, jumping from 38 to 383. With an electronic book, it's easy, but different.

✔ **Use the slider.** The slider, which you can see in Figure 9-11, comes up at the bottom of your eBook page if you tap the page. It's a blue horizontal line with a glowing dot somewhere along its path. The dot shows where you are in the book. Drag the slider right or left. If you're reading a book that someone has loaned you, a button at the right end of the slider lets you buy your own copy.

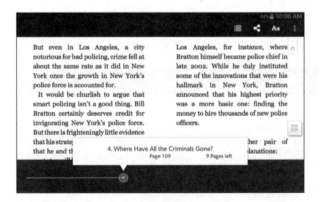

Figure 9-11: The slider appears at the bottom of a book if you tap anywhere on the page.

✔ **Enter a Jump To page number.** Follow these steps to quickly jump to a particular page in an eBook:

1. **Tap anywhere on the text.**

   The page slider appears.

2. **Tap the Menu icon in the upper right.**

3. **Tap the Jump to Page option.**

    A numeric keypad appears.

4. **Type a specific page number.**

    Page numbering is relative to the typeface, type size, and other design settings you have made.

Using tricky navigation

Maybe you don't know what page you want. Instead, you'd like to see the chapters in the table of contents. Or perhaps you'd like to search the book. Or you've decided that the typeface is too small or the page background is the wrong color. These are all fine thoughts, and with an electronic device like this one, your wishes are the NOOK's command.

To see the table of contents, or change the page's look, or to search the book, do this:

1. **Tap anywhere on the page of text.**

    The main reading tools open, including the slider.

2. **Tap an icon in the status bar: Contents, Share, Appearance, or Menu.**

Figure 9-12 points out the icons:

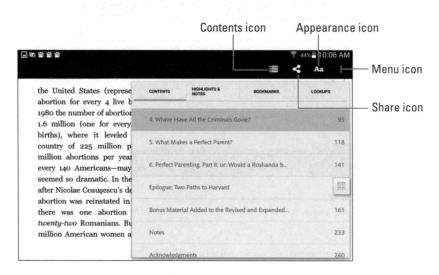

Figure 9-12: You can see a book's table of contents and easily jump to another section by tapping a chapter title.

✔ **Contents.** This icon is a stack of four horizontal dotted bars. When you tap the icon, you see four tabs at the top of the panel. I deal with each of them here.

- **Table of Contents.** The chapters are here, sometimes with subsections. You can scroll up or down through the listing, and best of all, the entries are active. The current chapter is highlighted by a gray bar. In most books you can jump immediately to a section by tapping the name.

- **Highlights and Notes.** The NOOK keeps track of your notes for you. And even better, you can jump to any note or highlight by tapping the item.

- **Bookmarks.** An electronic bookmark works just like a piece of cardboard between pages: It lets you quickly open to a particular page. You can set as many bookmarks as you like in each book.

- **Lookups.** Here you find any words you looked up in the electronic dictionary while reading this book. Tap a word to reread the meaning, as defined in itsy-bitsy *Merriam-Webster's Collegiate Dictionary,* Eleventh Edition.

✔ **Share.** Reading can be a solitary activity, but there's also a longstanding tradition of book clubs and sharing amongst friends. When you tap the Share icon, you see the choices shown in Figure 9-13:

- **Recommend.** Praise a book to friends and acquaintances by sending email, posting a recommendation on your Facebook wall (or that of a friend who granted you that permission), or tweeting through your Twitter account.

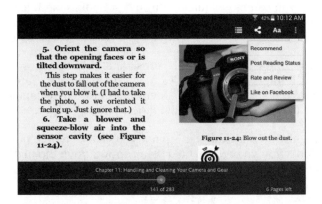

Figure 9-13: If you're a sharing, social type of reader, you can communicate with friends from the pages of a NOOK book.

• **Post Reading Status.** You can tell others how far you've gotten in the current book by posting a message on Facebook or Twitter. Why? I'm really not sure, but someone must be interested.

• **Rate and Review.** Send your comments and a 1–5 rating for display on www.BN.com, or post your review on Facebook or Twitter.

• **Like on Facebook.** Proclaim to the world (or at least those who read your Facebook news feed) that you really, really like this book.

Before you can use email or social network services, you have to link your NOOK to your Facebook or Twitter accounts or add email accounts to the Contacts app.

✔ **Appearance.** The Aa icon is how you change how your text looks. Choose from eight type sizes, six typefaces, three line spacing and three margin options, and six background color choices. I explain more about changing the appearance of text a bit later in this chapter.

✔ **Find in Book.** Tap the Menu icon and tap Find in Book to bring up a virtual keyboard with space to enter a word or phrase. Then tap the magnifying glass on the keyb͡ , ͡ designer seems to have mixed metaphors here).

To use the built-in d ͡ ͡ ͡aning of a word, press and hold on the word. To ͡ ͡ ͡ion, tap the A-Z icon when the definition pops up.

Using reading to͡

There's a whole other path͡ ͡ ͡d whistles. From the Reading Tools menu, you can move ͡ ͡ ͡ugh a book, search for something specific, share your knowledge, ͡ ͡ange the way the page looks. I call these the *secondary reading tools,* but actually they're part of the same toolkit.

To see the secondary reading tools, press and hold on a word or anywhere on the page. It might take a few tries to get the hang of it: Tapping brings up the full set of tools, including the slider bar. A more determined press and hold brings up the secondary reading tools shown in Figure 9-14.

The tool highlights a word if that's what you've touched; it highlights a nearby word if you've pressed on a blank spot. Above the highlight, you see the buttons described in the following sections:

✔ Highlight

✔ Add Note

✔ Share Quote

✔ Look Up

✔ Find in Book

Figure 9-14: Press and hold to reveal reading tools. I've highlighted a quote to send to anxious new puppy parents.

Highlight

To select a word, press and hold on a word; then lift your finger. The word is highlighted in blue, and you'll see a darker blue vertical bar on either side of it (unless you've chosen a different color theme for the page).

To expand the highlight, tap and then drag one of the vertical bars; this tool is called the Text Selection tool. When you lift your finger or fingers (you can use your thumb and pointing finger to cover more area), the Text Selection toolbar appears.

You can't directly print a passage from your Tab 4 NOOK, but here's what you can do: Select a passage and send it to yourself by email. Then use a computer and printer to make a hard copy.

Be sure you understand the proper use of citations if you're using part of a copyrighted book in an academic paper or a publication of your own.

Add Note

You can insert a comment (up to 512 characters) about the highlighted word or phrase; the date and time are included. A small icon that looks like a sticky note with a + mark will appear onscreen.

✔ You can search for what's in your note.

✔ You can view and change notes any time.

✔ You can make notes invisible. Why? Perhaps you want to share a selection or loan a book but keep your comments private.

To perform other actions on a note you've already made, use the primary reading tools. Here's how:

1. **Tap anywhere on the page.**

   The slider bar and system bar appear at the bottom of the page.

2. **Tap the Contents icon.**

   The icon looks like a stack of four dotted bars, and is pointed out in Figure 9-12.

3. **Tap the Highlights and Notes tab if it isn't already selected.**

4. **Tap one of the notes.**

   You're taken to the page where it's attached.

5. **Tap the highlighted word on the page.**

   A menu appears.

6. **Tap an option:**

   - **View Note.** Tap to read the comments you placed there.

   - **Edit Note.** Tap to see the comments onscreen. Use the keyboard to make changes. When you're done, tap Save.

   - **Remove Note.** Tap to delete the note; there's no second chance, so be sure this is what you want to do.

   - **Remove Highlight.** Tap to take away the color highlighting. The color shading disappears immediately, but you can always press on the word and reinstall a bit of a hue.

   - **Change Color.** Tap one of three colors (aqua, lime green, or sunset yellow) to make a change.

Share Quote

You can share a word or pick up a short passage and send it by email (or Twitter or in a Facebook post). The NOOK is ready, willing, and able to assist.

When you tap Share Quote, here are your choices:

- **To Contacts.** This sends the quote using the Email app to your saved contacts.

- **To My Facebook Wall.** Your erudite observations (or those of an accomplished author) are posted onto the pretend wall of your Facebook page, if you have one and have linked it to the NOOK system. (Earlier versions of the NOOK app allowed you to post your comments to a friend's Facebook wall; thankfully, that threat to our civil liberties and collective intelligence has been removed. Or perhaps they forgot to include it on the new model.)

- **Via Twitter.** Apparently the world is holding its breath, awaiting your latest observation of 140 characters or fewer; if you've linked your Twitter account, you can send a quote as a tweet to all of your followers.

Dog-earing a page

Back in ancient times, I used to tear up any old piece of paper I could find and insert it into the pages of a book I was reading. (I never could bring myself to crease the corners of a book or write in its pages. A book in my library, though read half a dozen times, still looks as pristine as the day it was bought.)

The following sections explain how modern folk bookmark an electronic publication.

- **Bookmark the page you're reading.** Tap in the upper-right corner of the page. A small blue ribbon appears in the corner of the page. To make the bookmark go away, tap the blue ribbon in the upper-right corner of the page.

- **See all the bookmarks in a book.** Follow these steps to see everything you've bookmarked:

    1. **Tap the center of the page to open the reading tools.**

    2. **Tap the Contents icon (pointed out in Figure 9-12).**

    3. **Tap the Bookmarks tab (in the Contents pane).**

        To jump to a bookmarked page, tap a bookmark in the list.

        Tap anywhere on the page *outside* the list of bookmarks to close the list.

✓ **Clear all bookmarks in a book.** Follow along to get rid of all the bookmarks in a single book:

1. **Tap the Contents icon (pointed out in Figure 9-12).**

2. **Tap the Bookmarks tab.**

3. **Tap Clear All.**

4. **Tap OK.**

Designing Your Own eBook

Gutenberg could never have imagined this. This menu, for reasons known only to the designers at B&N, has a different look and feel than most of the other options screens in the tablet. Never mind, though; it's pretty easy to use. See Figure 9-15, which shows the boxes.

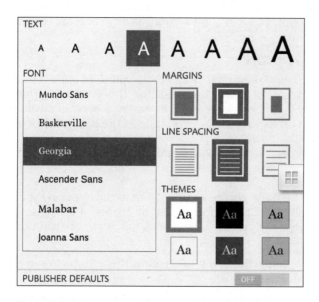

Figure 9-15: On one menu screen, you have dozens of combinations of fonts, type size, margins, line spacing, and themes.

✓ **Text.** In most eBooks you can choose from eight type sizes. Start out at the fifth or sixth largest for a good balance between readability and number of words that fit on the page. Feel free to experiment, though; tapping any of the As changes the size of the type that shows behind or above the menu.

- **Margins.** Experiment here between narrow, medium, and wide margins for the text. The more white space there is around the text, the fewer words will fit on each line.

- **Line Spacing.** You can adjust the amount of space between lines of text: single spacing, 1.5-line spacing, and double spacing.

- **Themes.** With an advanced eReader and a color LCD, you can choose the "paper" and the lighting. See Figure 9-15.

- **Font.** The Tab 4 NOOK comes with six different type styles. (Some book publishers may limit the options, though.) Feel free to experiment with the fonts to find one that's easiest to read.

- **Publisher Defaults.** Maybe you want to leave all of the decision making to a professional graphic designer. Drag the switch to On to use the formatting recommended by the publisher; you'll see the selections on the menu, but all other options will be unavailable.

I like to do my own book design. I generally prefer a serif font like Georgia, a medium size, and tight line spacing. And depending on how late in the day it is, I sometimes choose the Butter theme over Day.

Reading Brainy or Trashy: Flipping Through a Magazine

Magazines come in all shapes, sizes, and special designs. Their electronic formats vary greatly; the way you see pages may be different from one magazine to another. Some are even interactive.

Most magazines offer two views. You get to choose:

- **Page view** shows the entire page, including text and images.
- **Article view** shows text only.

Page view

This digital representation of the printed magazine has photographs, drawings, charts, and other elements. You'll see small images in the lower half of the screen. Page view is available in both portrait and landscape modes.

- To move through the magazine, swipe your finger along the thumbnail images.
- Tap a page to jump directly to it; a progress bar below the images shows where you are in the entire issue.

✔ To make the thumbnail images reappear, tap in the middle of the screen.

✔ As you read a page, tap the right side of the screen to move to the next page; tap the left side to go back a page.

Why is moving through a magazine different than flipping through a book? Good question. Magazine publishers use a different electronic design than book publishers.

Article view

This format shows articles with few (or no) illustrations or photos. You can scroll through the text as you would in a book.

You can go directly from article to article:

1. **Tap the center of the screen.**

2. **Tap the Contents icon at the bottom of the page.**

   The icon is pointed out in Figure 9-12.

3. **Tap the cover, table of contents, or specific article.**

Smell of the Ink: Reading a Newspaper

Whether you've downloaded a single issue or you subscribe, newspapers are on your Daily Shelf and on the Newsstand page of your library.

✔ To open a newspaper, tap its front page. When it opens, the front page shows headlines and one or two paragraphs from the start of major articles.

✔ To read an article in more depth, tap its headline or the first paragraphs.

✔ To share parts of an article, tap in the middle of the page. From the reading tools, choose Share or Notes (if the publisher has allowed those features).

✔ Bookmark a page by tapping in the upper-right corner of the page.

✔ To turn to the next page of a newspaper, do any of the following:

   • Tap along the right edge of the screen.

   • Swipe your finger from right to left across the screen.

   • Swipe your finger from low to high on the screen.

✔ To go back a page in a newspaper, do one of these actions:

   • Tap along the left edge of the screen.

   • Swipe your finger from left to right across the screen.

   • Swipe your finger from high to low on the screen.

You flip through the pages of a catalog just as you do through a magazine. I especially like using the page curl animation as I hunt for an especially sturdy pair of hiking boots; I'm in training for an expedition from my office to the harbor, a hike of just under a mile that includes a dirt road, a stretch of gravel, cobblestones, and, eventually the cold North Atlantic. I try, especially in winter, to stop short of the ocean.

Getting Kids into the Act: Picture Books

The Tab 4 NOOK offers some special features for young readers (and those of you who sit by their side as they discover the joys of reading). Some picture books have a bit of animation that you can set into motion by tapping the screen; others read aloud parts of the book. See Figure 9-16.

Figure 9-16: Kids' books include some of the most advanced interactive features on the NOOK.

Kids' books are special

Keep these picture book tips in mind:

- ✓ Enlarge a book by spreading with two fingers. This isn't available on all books.

- ✓ Tap the up arrow at the center bottom of the page to see *thumbnails* (small pictures) of each page in the book; scroll left or right through them and tap the page you want to visit. Or you can let a kid do it.

- ✓ Children's books open in landscape mode to better present the two-page spreads of most picture books.

- ✓ If the speaker is tough to hear, use two sets of earphones plugged into a splitter. Splitters are available at most electronics stores and shacks.

Choosing a reading style

Some children's books can narrate themselves. Others move. These special features appear only if the book includes them.

- ✔ **Read by Myself.** Just the words and pictures. Tap the blue button to open the book. Some special activities may be marked with a white star; tap the star to play. Better yet, let a kid tap the star.

- ✔ **Read to Me or Read and Play.** Read and Play books have audio tracks and interactive features marked with a white star. Tap the orange Read to Me button or the purple Read and Play buttons to hear the author or an actor read aloud.

  If you're enjoying a Read and Play book, you can turn the pages only by tapping the onscreen arrows. The pages won't turn if you tap them.

- ✔ **Read and Record.** Daddy or Mommy (or a child!) can become the voice of a book. Here's how:

  1. **Tap the cover of a kid's book that has the Read and Record feature.**

  2. **On the opening screen, tap the green Read and Record button.**

     The book opens to the first page. See Figure 9-17.

  3. **Tap the green Record button.**

     It changes to a Stop button. But don't stop.

  4. **Start reading.**

  5. **When you're done recording, tap the Stop button.**

Figure 9-17: Certain picture books allow you to record your own voice, or that of your child, reading the text.

Keep these general Read and Record tips in mind:

- ✔ The tiny hole on the right side of the Tab 4 NOOK, just above the Power/ Lock button, is the microphone. Don't cover it with your hand while you're recording.

- ✔ Hold the tablet about 15 inches away from your mouth.

- ✔ Try to record in a quiet place without background noise.

- ✔ To hear your recording right away, press the Play button. Press the Pause button when you're done listening.

- ✔ If you're a perfectionist (or if someone dropped a pile of plates while the microphone was on), press the Re-record button and do it again.

- ✔ To keep recording, swipe or tap to the next page and then tap the Record button.

- ✔ To stop recording, tap the Done button in the lower left. A screen asks you to choose a picture as a symbol. Type a name for the recording.

- ✔ To play a recording, open the book and tap the picture icon for the file you created.

- ✔ To re-record, change the name, or delete the audio file, tap the Edit button next to the picture icon and then choose the option you want.

Geeking Out about NOOK Comic Books

Pow! Oomph! Wow! The Tab 4 NOOK can display specially formatted NOOK comics in portrait or landscape mode. Moving within a NOOK comic book is very similar to the steps involved in NOOK Kids titles.

- ✔ Tap the cover of a comic book to open it. See Figure 9-18.

- ✔ Swipe left or right to go forward or back, or tap the right or left side of the page for the same effect.

- ✔ Tap in the center of the screen to bring up the reader tools, including small versions of the entire document. Tap any image to go directly to a particular page.

- ✔ To zoom in on text and images, double-tap or spread. Double-tap again to return the page to normal.

- ✔ Bookmark a page by tapping the + icon in the upper right. After you place a marker, tap the center of the page to see reader tools, tap the Contents icon (pointed out in Figure 9-12), and then tap the Bookmarks tab.

- ✔ Jump directly to any bookmarked page by tapping the bookmark.

Figure 9-18: DC Comics includes some fancy anthologies of classics, including a guide to Superman's backstory.

10

Finding Other eBook Sources

In This Chapter

▶ Investigating the Google Play Store

▶ Checking out the Amazon Kindle Store

▶ Using OverDrive

I'll say it one more time: Your Samsung Galaxy Tab 4 NOOK is a hybrid, kind of like a *liger* or a *tigon.* (Look them up on Google . . . .)

Your tablet has two more sources for books, magazines, newspapers, music, video, and apps, and you can add others. Explore them here in this chapter. And then it's your turn to go shopping.

Snooping around the Google Play Store

The Play Store is known as Google Play on Google-branded devices; it also had a former name, the Android Market. They are all the same: the official store for products to be used, read, watched, or listened to on a device running Android. See Figure 10-1.

The Play Store isn't playing around. It offers these categories: Books, Games, Movies & TV, Music, and Newsstand. By the time you read these words, the Play Store is likely to be approaching 2 million available apps, and tens of thousands of books and other media.

When you set up your Tab 4 NOOK (see Chapter 4), you were asked to link the tablet to an existing Google account or to create a new one. (Using an existing account lets you sync and share apps and some other materials.)

Throughout the store you'll find items for sale as well as free products. Why free? Some developers hope to make money by delivering space on your tablet to advertisers; others hope to entice you to pay to upgrade: Get more features! Buy other products! For example, in the Play Music store, you'll find individual tracks for sale as well as discounted or free tracks or entire albums. See Figure 10-2.

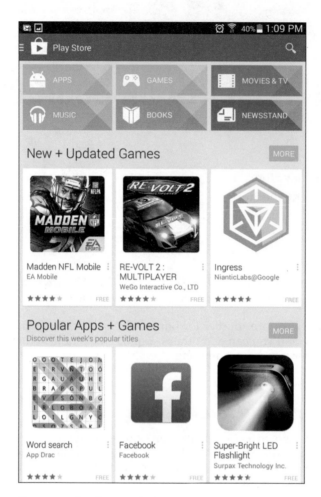

Figure 10-1: The Play Store offers apps, games, films, TV shows, music, books, and news.

Similarly, you'll find books under all sorts of pricing schemes in the Play Books store. The prices for books in the Play Books store are often the same as those in the NOOK Shop or the Amazon Kindle Store, but not always. If you're concerned about saving a dollar here and there (and why not) you can compare prices from the comfort of your sofa. See Figure 10-3.

Some publishers allow you to read free samples, while others will give away entire books in hopes of hooking you on a series. The hook-em-with-a-free-book scheme is especially popular with romance novels, which, when successful, tends to attract loyal and voracious readers.

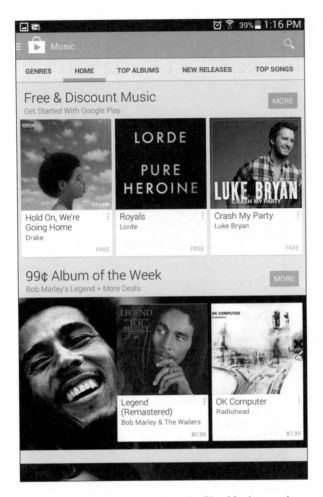

Figure 10-2: Anything you get from the Play Music store is on your tablet, and you can get to it through the Music app.

Play Books has an extensive collection of classic books, many of them for free or at very inexpensive prices. (The authors, most of them dead, receive no royalties.)

Google is a huge company now, and it — along with Amazon — has among the most experienced and creative marketers in the digital industry. The pages of the Play Store are very nicely designed and the buying process well thought out.

You can't loan titles you buy from Play Books to anyone; on this tablet only the NOOK Library is set up to do that. However, if you trust someone enough to allow the temporary relocation of your Tab 4 NOOK tablet, you can loan the device and the books (and other media) it contains. Be sure you're clear about your desire to get it back, though.

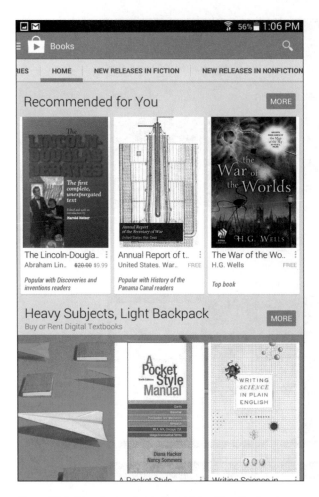

Figure 10-3: The electronic shelves of the Play Books store aren't quite as full as those in the NOOK Shop or the Kindle Store, but they have a strong selection.

The Play Movies & TV store has current titles (many sold in either SD, standard definition, or higher-priced HD, high definition). If you're only going to view the video on your Tab 4 NOOK, you might want to buy the SD version; on the small screen of your tablet the difference in resolution may not be noticeable.

You can also rent certain titles at a lower cost. Again, SD and HD versions are available. The amount of time and the conditions of rental can vary from studio to studio, so be sure to read the fine print before tapping Buy. Play Movies & TV has films, individual television shows, and entire seasons for sale or rent.

Also available through the Play Store are games, apps, magazines, and newspapers. See Figure 10-4. Prices for some magazines and newspapers are quite reasonable — well below the price you'd pay at a real newsstand. If you can find one.

Payment for items purchased from the Play Store can be by credit or debit card or through PayPal.

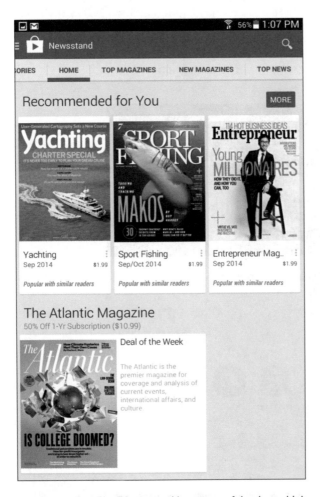

Figure 10-4: The Play Newsstand has news of the day, which might entice you to visit the shop regularly.

Samsung has free apps in the Galaxy Apps panel that appears on the Home screen of your Tab 4 NOOK tablet.

Taking the Kindle Store for a Spin

Amazon.com, which originally had been intended to be called Cadabra, has proved to be a nearly unstoppable force in digital merchandising since it sold its first item — a book — in 1995. Now Amazon sells just about everything, and its Kindle eBook system is a huge player in the industry.

Why am I talking about the Amazon Kindle in a book about a tablet marketed by Barnes & Noble to sell eBooks through its own NOOK division?

You can add a Kindle app to your tab 4 NOOK; it's free, right there in the Play Store. See Figure 10-5. You might need to install it on your tablet to be able to read Kindle-only library books that you borrow.

Figure 10-5: You can download and install a copy of Kindle for Android from the Google Play Store.

Although neither Google nor Barnes & Noble can be very happy about the presence of a third bookseller on a single tablet, as a consumer you can appreciate the wide choice. You can buy current and classic books from the Kindle, as well as a growing number of titles self-published by authors or provided by other sources specifically for the Kindle. And Amazon, a ferocious competitor, also has various offers including free books for members of its Amazon Prime service and other special promotions. See Figure 10-6.

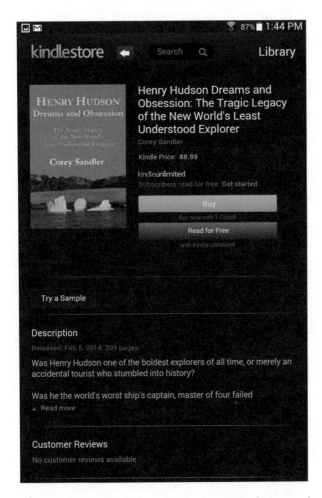

Figure 10-6: Kindle Unlimited lets members of the (extra-cost) Amazon Prime program borrow titles for reading.

Amazon, like Apple, is a very tightly controlling company. The book files it provides are stored in the company's proprietary format. What does that mean for you? Books you buy from Amazon have to be read using Amazon's own eReader, which does a fine job and works like the NOOK eReader.

Your NOOK books won't appear in the Kindle library and your Kindle books won't be on the shelves of your NOOK library.

Going in to OverDrive at the Library

I love libraries, and as a young man I once fulfilled several of my fantasies by dating a children's librarian (we both were of legal age). But I digress. Today's libraries are quite changed from what they were just a decade or so ago. You'll find free Wi-Fi and computer terminals, plus other electronic services. And many libraries now offer online loans of eBooks; all you need is a library card and the proper app. See Figure 10-7.

One of the leaders in library eBook management is OverDrive, which works with more than 27,000 libraries and schools and perhaps two million titles. You can get a copy of the OverDrive app from the Play Store.

Check with your local library to see if they participate, and see whether they're part of a network that includes other lenders in the region. Books are usually loaned over the Internet for one or two weeks, and most borrowers are limited to a set number of titles at a time. You don't have to drop the books off in a slot when they're due; the file disappears when it's due.

OverDrive has its own electronic reader system, and the reader is quite capable. Just as with the NOOK reader, when you return to OverDrive after closing the app, you're automatically taken to the last page you were reading.

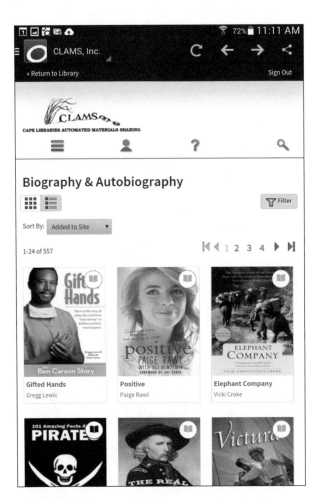

Figure 10-7: My Nantucket Atheneum is part of Cape Libraries Automated Materials Sharing (CLAMS); we've a lot of clams in the harbor, which we use for chowder.

Part IV
Throwing in the Kitchen Sink: Camera, Video, and Music

Take a perfect panoramic picture with help from www.dummies.com/extras/samnsunggalaxytab4nook.

In this part . . .

- Use the front and rear cameras.
- Organize pictures and videos in Gallery.
- Buy music by the track or album.
- Watch a movie or TV show.

11

Snapping Pictures

The Samsung Galaxy Tab 4 NOOK is essentially a midsized smartphone in many ways. And like any proper current smartphone, it has not one, but two cameras — one on the back and the other on the front. They can take still pictures or video.

I still laugh when I see people holding a tablet at arm's length and tapping at the screen to take a picture. It's a bit awkward and hard to control. But still, it's a camera and the result is still a photograph.

Putting Down a Book to Take a Picture

On the plus side, the cameras in this NOOK can immediately display the pictures or videos you make (and with a screen considerably larger than the ones on plain old digital cameras). You can create a gallery of images on the tablet and do some basic editing, and you can share them by email, social network, or Internet.

The absence of a flash or LED light isn't a big deal in most situations. Use the sun outside or a lamp indoors to light your subject. And here are a pair of tips to help with faces or details: Outdoors, have an assistant hold a white card or something similar to reflect sunlight onto a face. Indoors, turn up the lights and have someone standing outside of the image aiming a light at faces.

On the Internet, you can upload or transfer your files to a photo printing service and get decent prints. Think small: a 4x6-inch or 5x7-inch print should be sharp and pleasing. Larger than that, not so much.

Thinking about yourselfie

We are in the Age of the Selfie. For reasons that I completely fail to understand, youngsters (of all ages) seem to have adopted the practice of holding their tablet or smartphone at arm's length in front of them and taking a picture — of themselves in front of a landmark, or of themselves with friends and family, or of themselves with a meal. In some situations the selfie has essentially replaced the old-fashioned concept of collecting an autograph from a celebrity. (I don't understand autograph hunting, either, so feel free to officially declare me a very computer, camera, and tablet-savvy old fogy.)

The front camera takes and store your selfie as a photo. At its 1.3 megapixel resolution, it will work for profile pictures and for small prints of perhaps 4x6 inches. Enjoy.

Taking a Camera Tour

In Figure 11-1 you can see the basic camera controls. Let me go through them briefly here, and then you can examine them in more detail later in the chapter.

- Starting in the upper left corner, tap the Mode icon to see exposure presets.

- The white box with four gray squares is the Quick menu, an optional feature I enabled to allow rapid access to certain apps and commands; you can enable this through the Accessibility features in Settings. (You can get one for yourself in Chapter 4.)

- The large icon with an image of a camera is the shutter. Tap it to take a picture.

- Below the shutter is an oblong icon that in Figure 11-1 is currently set to the still camera; if you touch and move up or down, you can change it to video camera.

- At bottom left is an indication of the current Mode setting. In this case it's Auto.

- At the top center of the screen is a down arrow. Tap the icon to display a choice of filters, available only on the rear-facing camera.

- At upper right is a small square that is a quick path to the Gallery. Tap here to see the most recently taken photo as well as all others stored on the device.

You can share images right from the Camera app. When an image is in the Review screen, tap the > icon and choose Share.

✔ At bottom right is a set of additional controls. Tap the Settings (gear) icon to see adjustments, including photo size (resolution), metering (how much light gets in), and other custom settings.

✔ Switch between the rear- and front-facing camera by tapping the icon showing a camera with left and right arrows. Use the back camera (on the opposite side of the screen) for landscapes and portraits. Use the front-facing camera (used for video calls and *selfies* — self portraits.)

✔ The left-facing arrow opens a few other controls, including a self-timer, exposure adjustment, and automatic image sharing. As shown in Figure 11-1, I haven't tapped the arrow. You see two icons that indicate that the GPS or location services feature is on (pictures can include location information) and that images are being stored on the microSDHC card.

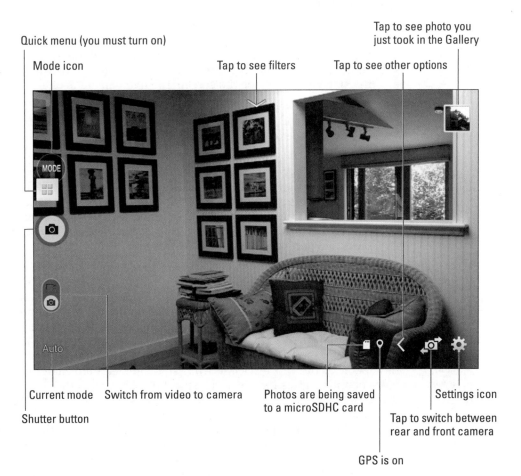

Quick menu (you must turn on)

Mode icon

Tap to see filters

Tap to see other options

Tap to see photo you just took in the Gallery

Current mode   Switch from video to camera

Shutter button

Photos are being saved to a microSDHC card

Settings icon

Tap to switch between rear and front camera

GPS is on

Figure 11-1: The basic camera controls for the Samsung Galaxy Tab 4 NOOK.

Tap-Clicking with a Tablet

Are you ready to use your tablet as a camera? From the Home screen, scroll through the app icons on the lower portion of the screen; tap the Camera icon. Or, you can tap the Apps icon on the Home screen and find a Camera icon there.

After a brief interlude during which the tablet changes its personality, you see the main camera screen, as you've already seen in Figure 11-1. Tap the shutter to grab a photograph. But before then:

- You can hold your tablet camera in either landscape (wider than tall) or portrait orientation (taller than wide). The buttons and controls will stay where they are on the screen, but their labels will rotate as you turn the tablet between aspects.

- To tell which camera you're using, look at the screen. If you see whatever's in front of the tablet, you're using the rear camera. Some of you are already starting to drift off into Alice in Wonderland confusion, I'm sure. Remember that the *front* camera is the one on the front, which is the side you use to see the screen; the *rear* camera is on the back.

- To switch between the front and rear camera, tap the icon of a camera that has left and right arrows. Each time you tap it, you switch between one lens or the other. If you see your own face, tap once to use the rear camera.

- If the tiny lens on the back or front of the tablet gets dirty, your pictures are going to appear smudged or otherwise less-than-lovely. Gently clean the lens with a soft cloth or a tissue. If the lens has some sticky gunk on its face, you can *slightly* moisten the cloth with just a *bit* of water, or a lens-cleaning solution like the ones used for eyeglasses. Don't press hard, and don't assault the lens with a nail file or jackhammer.

- On the screen, tap the spot you want to focus on. In certain combinations of light and modes, you may be able to shift the point of focus slightly. For example, if you're taking a picture of a person standing in front of a field of sunflowers, tap that person's face so that he or she is in focus. Or, tap a distant sunflower to emphasize the beauty of nature over your friend's face.

As capable as the Tab 4 NOOK is, this isn't a full-featured camera with a fine piece of optical glass for a lens. The fixed plastic lens on the tablet — like those on nearly every tablet and smartphone — is best suited to put nearly everything in focus in a well-lit setting. For those of you who are experienced photographers: The aperture isn't adjustable, and therefore the depth of field doesn't vary. All photos are taken at an aperture of f2.6; to compensate for extremes of light or lack of light, the tablet can boost or reduce the electronic shutter speed and turn up or turn down the sensitivity of the sensor.

You'll see a short lag between the moment you tap the shutter and when the photo's recorded. This is the price we pay for all of the automated functions that are handled for you by the tablet camera: exposure calculation, white balance adjustment, and autofocus. This makes it a little more difficult to take action photos; practice a bit to learn how to anticipate motion. And don't hesitate to reshoot if you find that someone has closed his eyes or made a face.

Zooming in for a Close-up

I'm determined to give you the whole truth and nothing but the truth, so help me NOOK. And so here are two observations about the zoom effect on the cameras of your tablet:

- Before taking a photo, you can zoom in as much as four times by pressing the Volume key up or down on the side of the tablet.
- You may well wish you hadn't.

Here's why: There's *no* zoom lens on this tablet (or any other consumer tablet). Instead, the electronics enlarge part of the image. It's called a *digital zoom.* See Figure 11-2. (Digital SLR cameras have the other kind of enlargement: *optical zoom.*)

 To put things in perspective (a little photographic joke there), your Tab 4 NOOK tablet can work pretty well for snapshots and landscapes. But don't expect its quality to come anywhere near that of even the most basic digital camera, and it's not even in the ballpark if you're comparing it to a professional SLR with a huge lens (and an owner with a backache).

Figure 11-2: The Volume key on the side of the tablet can zoom you in or out; which reduces the quality of your picture.

Changing the Resolution

You can adjust the Galaxy Tab's rear camera sensor's resolution, up to 3 megapixels (MP); the front camera has a maximum resolution of 1MP. The higher the resolution you use, the more detail is recorded. If you want to send the video as an email attachment or to otherwise upload your movie to the Internet or to another device, a large file may take quite a while to transmit. Some email services may even reject attempts to send very large files.

Chapter 12 explores the Gallery app in more detail. In the Gallery you can review, organize, share, and perform basic editing on still pictures and videos.

Although it essentially means the same thing, Samsung changed the name from Resolution to Photo Size. To set the rear camera's resolution before you take a photo, do this:

1. **With the Camera app open, tap the Settings (gear) icon.**

2. **If the Image tab isn't already selected, tap it.**

3. **Choose Photo Size.**

4. **Select a resolution:**

   - **2048x1536 (4:3).** This is the largest image file, just over 3 megapixels and available only on the rear camera.

   - **2048x1152 (16:9).** About 2.3 megapixels, this aspect ratio is used in HD flat-screen TVs. Rear camera only.

   - **1600x1200 (4:3).** About 1.9 megapixels, in the more squarish 4:3 ratio. Rear camera only.

   - **1280x720 (16:9).** About .9 megapixel, in an HD-like elongated shape. Front and rear cameras.

   - **640x480 (4:3).** The smallest, lowest resolution setting for the rear camera, about .3 megapixel. Though small, this size is fine for small images used as profile pictures on LinkedIn or Facebook. Front and rear cameras.

   See Figure 11-3.

5. **Tap outside the menu to return to the Camera app.**

You can shoot an image at high resolution and later send a smaller file as an email attachment. Visit the Google Play Store for free or paid apps that let you adjust the file size. Save a copy of the picture with a different name; that way you have the high-resolution image and a smaller file to share.

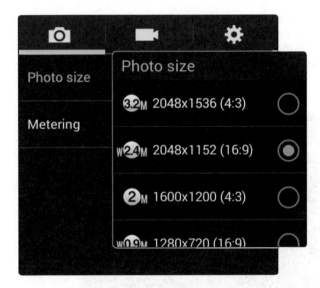

Figure 11-3: Choose from five photo sizes or resolutions for the rear-facing camera, and two lesser resolutions for the front camera.

Setting Up Picture Preferences

"Film" is free on a digital camera. Experiment with the various configurations and settings to get the best possible pictures from your tablet camera.

Your tablet camera can hold thousands, or even tens of thousands, of photos — especially if you expand its memory by installing a microSD card. Remember, too, that the higher the resolution you use, the more storage space you need. You can change a resolution setting. The math is pretty straightforward: Reducing the resolution by half allows twice as many files to be stored.

You can mess around with these camera settings:

✔ **Metering:** Your tablet adjusts itself to make the best possible exposure, adjusting the *shutter speed* (the amount of time the sensor records light) as well as the sensitivity of the sensor itself. But your Galaxy Tab 4 NOOK (and even professional photo gear) can become confused in a situation that has a wide range of light levels in the same scene: for example, a sunny day at the beach with deep shadows under umbrellas and extreme highlights dancing on the surf. Doesn't this make you want to head for the shore right now? I'll be back in a moment after I ride a few waves. Meanwhile, consult Figure 11-4.

• **Center-Weighted** makes exposure decisions based on the lighting conditions in the middle of the scene. If you choose this option, put the most essential element of your picture in the middle of the image; that's not always the most aesthetically pleasing composition, but you can always crop the image later.

Figure 11-4: The basic camera controls for the Samsung Galaxy Tab 4 NOOK.

• **Matrix**, as far as I'm aware, has nothing whatsoever to do with Keanu Reeves and an artificial reality that's set up to control human minds. The Matrix setting averages out the entire scene to come up with the best exposure setting. This works well when the range of light is consistent: in other words, scenes where the darkest dark and lightest light aren't all that far apart.

• **Spot** is a good one for attentive, patient photographers. The tablet sets the exposure based on wherever you tap the image. The trick is to find a place that's best for the image you want to record. Tap a face to expose best for that part of the picture, for example.

✔ **Brightness.** You can manually adjust the amount of light that gets in. Photographers call this the *exposure value (EV)*. You can turn *down* the setting for a super-bright beach scene, or turn it up for low-light situations. Either way, you're going against the tablet camera's automatic exposure setting; again, experiment with the setting if your pictures are overall too dark or too light. See Figure 11-5.

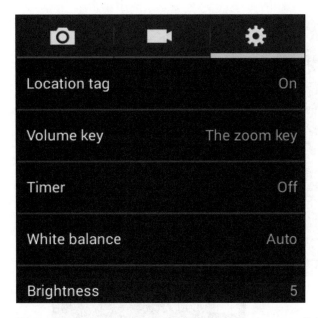

Figure 11-5: You can turn on (or off) the location tag, set a self-timer, and adjust white balance, brightness, or exposure value.

The tablet's brightness levels run between 1 (darkest) to 9 (lightest). Think of it this way: 9 is the largest amount of brightness in the image. Going all the way to 9 will *blow out* or *clip* the highlights, reducing detail in very bright spots; going down to 1 will underexpose dark areas, dropping detail there. Use this adjustment carefully, and review your results immediately after taking a picture to see if it came out how you want.

✓ **White Balance.** Here the available choices: Auto, Daylight, Cloudy, Incandescent, or Fluorescent. Think about the difference in the color of light at midday when it's toward blue, or at sunset when light's more orange or even red. The same applies to indoor settings: Candlelight is red-orange, while a standard fluorescent bulb is much cooler, toward blue. Your tablet, like all digital cameras, can automatically search out pure white, but you might want to experiment with manually setting the white balance, either to get a more accurate image or to create an artistic view. Experiment. See Figure 11-6.

✓ **Location Tag:** You generally know where you are. And your Samsung Galaxy Tab 4 NOOK usually does as well, using its built-in GPS receiver. Which raises the question: Do you want your pictures to include a GPS location tag?

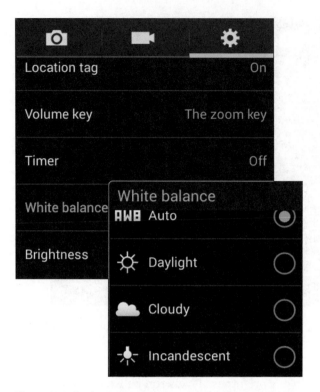

Figure 11-6: Setting white balance might be helpful in a room with mixed lighting, such as a room lit with lightbulbs but also by daylight through a window.

The strength and accuracy of GPS signals can vary from place to place. Sometimes they're weak inside buildings, or in areas between buildings where the view of the horizon is blocked. Weather conditions can also affect GPS signals. If you leave Location Tag turned on, the tablet applies the last good signal it had to your photos, updating your position any time it can.

In a perfect world, most of us would say, "Yes, of course. What a nifty special feature." But some people worry about privacy. What if that picture ended up in the hands of someone else — someone you don't want to know where you were when you took the picture? If you send your pictures to someone else by email, or especially if you upload them to the Internet, you lose control over whatever information is embedded in the file.

Speaking for myself, I think the advantage of having a GPS location in a photo file far outweighs any possible loss of privacy. But you'll have to make that decision for yourself. If you don't want location tags in your images, turn off that setting.

✔ **Guidelines.** This one, for me, is an essential. Turn on guidelines to have the tablet draw a grid on the screen. Use the grid to keep horizons or buildings upright or perpendicular; guidelines are especially useful when you are holding a thin, flat rectangular tablet camera at arm's length.

Choosing camera modes and filters

Somewhere out there is someone who's never adjusted the color settings on a television set, never boosted the bass on a car radio, and never chosen to add a pinch of oregano to a plate of lasagna. But we're not like that, right? We like to live life to the fullest. We *customize*.

That's one of the beauties of working with a computer, or in your case a tablet. Although you can work entirely with the camera's settings as delivered from the factory, you can select hundreds of combinations of modes to make your Galaxy Tab 4 NOOK your very own.

The selections you can make include

✔ **Modes.** Exposure changes for high-speed sports, close-up faces, or night scenes and the like. See Figure 11-7.

✔ **Filters.** Changes to the color model.

Figure 11-7: Choosing certain modes lets you tinker with the shutter speed and the sensitivity of the sensor.

Modes

To set modes, tap the indicator in the upper-right corner of the camera screen. Not all modes are available on both the front and rear cameras:

✔ **Auto:** This is the *point-and-shoot* option, which means the tablet chooses the best settings. Sometimes it works great; sometimes it sees the world completely differently than you do. But we're smarter than a machine . . . sometimes.

✔ **Beauty Face:** A makeover without makeup or surgery. This mode looks for faces in the image and softens and smooths the skin. It works better in close-up portraits than in distant images, and some results are better than others. Give it a try.

✔ **Night:** If you want to try a night scene using available light — without a flash — try this mode. Keep the tablet as still as possible while the picture is taken. Because the sensor's sensitivity might be boosted, you could wind up with a lower-quality image. But it's a mode worth a bit of experimenting.

✔ **Panorama:** Use the tablet's brain to stitch together multiple photos into one large panoramic image. Brace yourself and keep the tablet as steady as you can as you slowly move it in an arc from left to right, or right to left.

You'll see a blue guide frame on the screen; when you move the tablet so that it fills the guide frame, it takes the next picture in the series. To stop shooting the pano, tap the Stop (square) icon. Panorama mode automatically stops if it can't recognize elements of the previous picture.

Panoramas work best when there are simple but recognizable backgrounds, like trees or windows. Shooting against empty skies or blank walls may confuse the camera, which may confuse the image, which will confuse you when you try to make sense of what you've got.

✔ **Sound & Shot:** This is like a video, only without the moving picture. Select this option to take a *still* photo that has a few seconds of audio attached to the file. For example, you can dictate a note to yourself as you take a picture. "This is the Altar of Zeus at the Acropolis of Pergamon," you might say, if you happened to be shooting a picture standing near the river Bakırçay in western Turkey.

✔ **Sports:** This mode makes the camera shoot as fast (or short) a shutter time as possible. If the lighting's good, this may be enough to capture a moving object — a baseball player sliding into home plate or that cat falling off the refrigerator again.

Forcing the camera to use a fast shutter means that less light reaches the sensor. The same goes for forcing the camera to turn off the flash even in low light. The Samsung Galaxy Tab 4 NOOK has a *fixed aperture*, meaning that you can't adjust the lens opening. And so, your tablet has to make up for a fast exposure or low light by boosting the sensitivity of the sensor. If you have a brightly lit scene, all will be well; if the lighting is less than great, the image quality will suffer. In the worst of situations, your great sports scene might look like it was photographed through a milkshake.

If you press the Power key while you're using the Camera app, the screen will lock, basically disabling the shutter while keeping in place all adjustments and settings you have made. When you're ready to take pictures, press the Power key once again to unlock the camera.

Filters

Your tablet offers filters, and not all are offered in each mode (or on each camera, front and rear). They can be fun to play around with, but you might be better off shooting your pictures in full color and then applying color filters or modifications using a photo editing program on a desktop or laptop computer.

Here's why: If you take a photo as a grayscale, the color is forever gone. If you shoot in color and edit a *copy* of that file, you can make all of the modifications you want and retain the original.

To turn off a filter effect, tap Normal:

- **Negative.** Black is white, white is black, and colors are presented as a digital equivalent of complementary hues. For example, red is green and blue is orange. See Figure 11-8.

- **Grayscale.** All color is stripped out of the file, and the image is shades of gray, with pure white and pure black as extremes.

- **Sepia.** This is a version of grayscale, but the overall image has a reddish-brown tone; it's like an old-fashioned style that's warmer than a black-and-white photo.

Figure 11-8: The negative filter on a color scene swaps colors. A well-exposed, well-composed black-and-white or grayscale photo is a work of art.

Here's why I don't use these filters: I want my camera — any camera — to capture as much information as possible. I can always convert a file to gray-scale, sepia tone, or other effects in Photoshop or Aperture. I keep the original image and change a copy of the file.

Customizing filenames and storage

An external microSDHC memory card in your tablet is a good place to store photographs. It leaves room for apps on the tablet's built-in memory.

Here's where you can use the power of your tablet's little computer to help you organize and store your images.

✓ **Contextual Filename:** If you turn on this feature *and* enable GPS location tagging, pictures and videos you take with your tablet camera will use GPS information. Photos I took while testing the tablet were named with the date, time, and the name of the street where my office is located. See Figure 11-9.

Figure 11-9: A contextual filename requires you to turn on GPS location tagging.

✓ **Volume Key:** You can assign a special function to the Volume key (on the side of your tablet) anytime you use the Camera app. Your options are

• **Zoom Key.** Pressing the + or – side of the Volume key zooms you in or out; your Volume key is set up this way already.

- **Cam/Rec Key.** If you make the Volume key work as a record key, pressing it in the Camera app takes a photo or starts (and stops) recording a video.

✔ **Timer:** You could probably guess the purpose of this setting, but after then you'll have to find a use for it. You can snap a photo after 2, 5, or 10 seconds. If you can prop your tablet upright, or place it in a stand of some sort, you could use this as a self-timer to allow you to get into the scene. Or you might experiment with having the tablet take a candid camera shot all by itself.

Be careful about propping your tablet and then running off to try to get into a photograph. You don't want the tablet to tumble.

✔ **Save as Flipped:** Here's a valuable setting that is a bit of a head-scratcher until your figure it out. This option's available only when you're using the front camera, the one that faces toward you when you're looking at the screen. It flips captured photos horizontally to correct for the mirror effect of the front camera. You do realize that the image you see of yourself in a mirror is flipped from the way others view you, right? Ponder on that for a while.

✔ **Storage:** If you install a microSD card in your Samsung Galaxy Tab 4 NOOK (which I recommend you do), here is where you can tell the tablet where you want your photos and videos stored.

In general, you should store your photos, videos, music, text files, and the like on the memory card and leave the built-in memory for apps. See Figure 11-10.

Figure 11-10: Tell the tablet where to store your photos. If you can, put them on a microSD card.

✔ **Reset:** If you've made adjustments of any sort to your camera — and I hope you will — you can quickly return all of them to the original settings — like when first you unboxed your Samsung Galaxy Tab 4 NOOK. This is an all-or-nothing reset, and it only affects camera settings.

 ✔ **Help:** Hmmm. What could this be? You can get some basic assistance in understanding the settings and modes for your tablet camera. If I might be so bold: The instructions here on the camera, like those in the manual supplied with it, aren't always all that helpful. But that's why you're reading these words in *Samsung Galaxy Tab 4 NOOK For Dummies.*

Making Movies

Tablet, camera, action!

The further you get into digital photography, the harder it is to remember that a video (or to use that old-fashioned word, a *movie*) is made up of hundreds or thousands or millions of individual still pictures. In the time of film, the movie would move through a projector and each still frame would have its moment on the screen. (Most motion pictures, to use another term, projected still frames at a rate of 24 per second.)

Video doesn't use film, of course, but the same principle applies. When you watch a video on TV, a tablet, or in a state-of-the-art movie theater, you're seeing individual still frames that are retrieved by the microprocessor from memory and then replaced by the next one in a series. On the Samsung Galaxy Tab 4 NOOK, the video frame rate is 30 per second.

The standard setting for the rear camera is high (or normal) resolution. The Samsung Galaxy Tab 4 NOOK uses the MP4 file format for videos.

Stubborn sight

The human brain is an amazingly sophisticated computer, more capable in many ways than the most advanced digital device. But the reason we're able to enjoy movies or videos is related to several optical illusions caused by the reaction speed of our brains. First is *persistence of vision,* which causes an afterimage to remain on the eye's retina (the equivalent of a digital camera's sensor) for approximately 1/25 of a second. If another image appears within that time period or less, the human brain doesn't notice a gap. The other optical illusion is called the *phi phenomenon,* which causes us to perceive continuous motion when objects move rapidly from frame to frame.

Recording video

You can only use the rear camera, the one facing away from the screen, to record videos.

To make your own video, do this:

1. **Open the Camera app.**

2. **From the main screen, drag the Camera icon so it changes to a Video Camera icon.**

   If you most recently used your camera for video, the icon should already display the video icon.

3. **To start making a video, tap the Record (red dot) icon.**

   You can momentarily halt recording by tapping Pause or

4. **Tap the Stop (square) icon when you're done.**

Keep these things in mind when you're recording:

- ✔ Hold the camera tablet as steady as you can. Bring your elbows in to your chest.

- ✔ If you plan on *panning* (moving left or right, or vertically), do so slowly and smoothly.

- ✔ Record in a well-lit setting: outdoors in daylight or using lamps indoors. You can, though, turn on the "flash" to record indoors.

- ✔ Be aware that keeping the flash LED light on for an extended period uses a lot of battery power.

Zooming in or out

While using the video camera, you can zoom in or out to make distant people or objects appear closer or return to the normal view. There are two ways to zoom:

- ✔ Use the Volume key on the side of the tablet to zoom in or out.

- ✔ Touch two fingers on an image and then spread them apart to zoom in. Bring the two fingers toward each other (pinch) to zoom out.

Extreme zooms are pretty poor quality. Judge for yourself whether a video (or camera) zoom is acceptable.

After you record a video, you can

- Review it by tapping the Gallery window within the camera screen.
- Close the Camera app and tap the Gallery app icon from the Home screen.

There you'll see a collection of both still and video files. Tap any thumbnail (small picture) to view.

12

Getting into the Gallery

Most of us have one: a box stuffed with hundreds of precious, irreplaceable family photographs. One of these days, I promise, I'll get around to sorting through them. Is that Aunt Ruth or Uncle Frank? They look so much alike. Was this picture taken at Orchard Beach, Brighton Beach, or Lake Maxinkuckee? And what do I do to separate out 73 hours of video of the kids arguing with each other from a few wonderful glimpses of cuteness?

Good luck with that project. I hope you complete it before the prints and film molder away.

But on a happier note, your Samsung Galaxy Tab 4 NOOK has features that help you organize, label, and share your photos and videos. It all comes together in a place called the Gallery.

Visiting Your Picture Gallery

Like the smart little computer it is, your Samsung Galaxy Tab 4 NOOK is available any time you need help, never takes a coffee break, and doesn't care if you stomp your feet and whistle as you browse the collection.

You can see any picture or video (including any you download from the Internet or email, or transfer from a computer) in the Gallery app. Visit the Gallery from the Home screen. Tap the Apps panel and tap Gallery. Or even quicker, tap the Gallery app icon in the lower part of the Home screen.

Going to the Gallery in this fashion brings up a screen showing all your image folders, including pictures you took on the tablet, screen captures (pictures of what's onscreen), and pictures or videos you've downloaded to the tablet from other sources such as from a desktop, laptop, or smartphone. See Figure 12-1.

Figure 12-1: A selection of albums in the Gallery's left panel and individual images in the right panel.

 Jump to the Gallery from the Camera app by tapping the preview box that appears in the corners of the camera. The images shown in the preview are *only* those you photographed using your Tab 4 NOOK. (You can see the Gallery icon pointed out back in Figure 11-1.)

 Your Tab 4 NOOK can only create and display certain file types. For still images taken with the camera, pictures use the JPG (pronounced by techies as *jay-peg*) format, a technology that squashes the size of the file with little or no loss of quality. Camera images are stored in the DCIM/Camera folder.

Screen captures use a file format called PNG (pronounced *ping*) which also squashes files without loss of quality; they're stored in a folder cleverly called Screen Captures.

You can transfer files, from another device, that are in a different format, but you get an error message when you try to see them, or they may appear damaged. Here's a way around: Convert incompatible file formats using a photo or video editing program on your PC or Mac before transferring them to your Tab 4 NOOK.

I sometimes use a tablet as a storage place for extra copies of important files I take with me when I travel. In that instance, it doesn't matter whether the tablet can display the incompatible format (including TIFF or RAW camera files); all I need to do in an emergency is get to a PC or laptop and upload the files to a computer that can handle them.

Viewing images

You want to see what pictures you have? Images are displayed in order of creation date.

- Tap a folder to open it and check its contents.
- Tap an image to view it full screen.
- Scroll left or right with your finger to view the previous or next image.

Zooming in or out

You can enlarge most images on the screen to take a closer look. You can zoom two ways:

- Double-tap anywhere on the screen to zoom in. Double-tap again to zoom out to normal view.
- Touch two fingers on an image and then spread them apart to zoom in. Bring the two fingers toward each other *(pinch)* to zoom out.

Deleting images

Film is all but gone, and taking pictures is all but free. But you don't need (or want) to hold on to every last image you record.

To delete an image from within the Gallery, follow along:

1. **With a folder open, tap the Menu icon.**
2. **Choose Select Item.**

3. **Tap a check mark in the image you want to can.**

4. **Tap the Delete (trash can) icon.**

   Or, while viewing an individual image, tap the Delete icon.

Putting All Your Pictures in One Basket

If you're the sort who likes to neatly separate all of your pictures or videos into folders that you name, that's fine. But you can also tell the Tab 4 NOOK tablet to do a bit of sorting: The most basic way is to show folders by date or by alphabetic order.

The tablet comes with some preset albums. Think of them as folders. But you can easily

✔ Create your own album while you're in the Gallery on the tablet.

✔ Add a folder (which is treated as an album) while using a PC or laptop computer to work in the files on your tablet.

I explain how to create folders and transfer files using a computer connected by the USB cable in Chapter 5.

To create an album from the Gallery app, do this:

1. **Tap the folder icon.**

   It's a small drawing of a folder with a +. It's in the upper right.

2. **Type a name for the album.**

3. **Tap OK. See Figure 12-2.**

   The new album or folder invites you to Drag Here. This has nothing whatsoever to do with your choice of clothing; it's an invitation to display an image that's shown elsewhere in your Gallery.

4. **Touch and hold your finger on the image for a second or two.**

   It'll start pulsing.

5. **Drag it into the new folder.**

6. **When you're finished, tap Done.**

7. **Choose an option:**

   • Move the picture to its new location.

   • Move a *copy* of the picture to the new location and leave the original where it is.

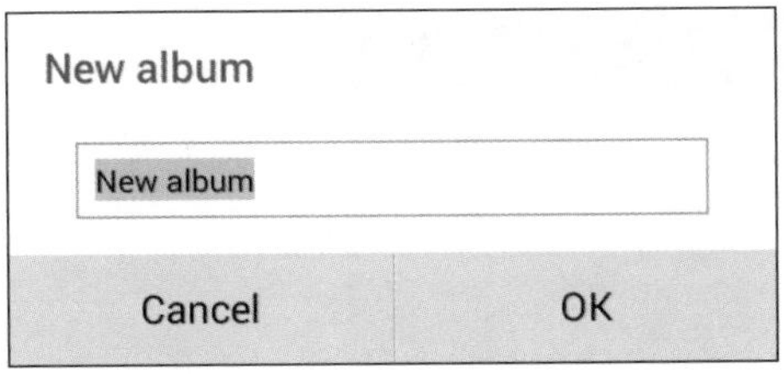

New album

New album

Cancel   OK

Figure 12-2: You can use preset album names, or create albums or folders of your own.

Sorting Your Pictures

You can examine photos, videos, and other images in ways that Marion the Librarian could never have imagined. Sort to your heart's content:

1. **From the main Gallery screen, tap Albums.**

   A submenu opens.

2. **Choose how you want your pictures sorted:**

   - **All.** You got this, right?

   - **Albums.** Show the names and the first image in each album.

   - **Time.** The oldest are at the top and most recent are at the bottom. You can scroll through all of the pictures by touching and sliding anywhere on the screen. Tap a single picture to see it full screen. Tap the Back icon to return to the display of images by time.

   - **Locations.** If you turn on your tablet's Locations feature, every photo and video you shoot will use the built-in GPS to figure out where it was taken. (I discuss this in more detail in Chapter 11.) And then you can tell the tablet: "Show me only the pictures taken on Nantucket Island." You can even display a map to see pins for all photos and videos that have this information. Tap a city, state, or country to see images from that place only. See Figure 12-3.

   - **People.** If you name faces using the Tag Buddy feature (I explain that next), the Tab 4 NOOK shows you those people.

   - **Favorites.** If you declare an image to be a favorite (tap the Menu icon in the upper right and then tap Favorite), selecting this method means only your favorites will show up.

Figure 12-3: While I was busy testing the camera outside of my office, the tablet figured out my latitude and longitude.

Tagging Your Buddies

Here's another technology to wrap your mind around: face tagging. No, it doesn't involve spray paint. You leave that up to your tablet. The feature's called Tag Buddy, but some online and onscreen manuals call it Face Tag. Same thing either way.

The feature uses information from your Contacts app, as well as your social media connections. You can also import your contacts from a PC or Mac.

Face tags stay on your tablet. When you share your pictures, people can't see the tags.

Turning on Tag Buddy

But first, you have to turn on Tag Buddy:

1. **Start the Gallery app.**

2. **Tap the Menu icon and choose Settings.**

3. **Slide the Tag Buddy switch to On.**

Tagging photos in the Gallery

You can troll through the Gallery and look for some faces amongst the pictures that are already there. When your tablet detects a recognizable face, it puts a yellow box around the face.

1. **(Optional) Resize the box a bit.**

   Your goal should be to neatly surround the face and exclude other distractions. It's possible to have two or more recognizable faces in a photo, and so you'll have two boxes to label.

2. **Tap Save.**

   You're asked which contact to assign to the face; if no tag exists, you can create one now.

3. **Tap the contact to associate it with the image.**

   Follow the onscreen instructions to share the image by email or social app if you choose.

When you use the tablet to take a photo, or import a photo onto your tablet, the system tries to match a face with one you've already tagged. But wait, there's more: If Locations is on, the tablet also includes that in the tag. And if the tablet was using its Wi-Fi connection, the Tab 4 NOOK will briefly glance at the weather. The result could be a tag that says when and where and who and a brief summary of the weather: "Me, Nantucket, and a Sunny day."

You can even take a photo of a photo; I tagged my all-time favorite family picture, a nearly 40-year-old portrait of me and the woman who was about to become my bride. She still looks young and lovely; I've gotten much older and hairier on the face, less hairy on top. See Figure 12-4.

If you've got the geeky nerve, here's a clever way to help you remember the names of people you meet at parties, weddings, conventions, or your first day at a new job. Take pictures of people and tag them; while you're at it, create a Contacts app listing with phone number, email, and notes.

Figure 12-4: Once a photo has been tagged, you're reminded of the names of the people when you view the photo on your Tab 4 NOOK.

Putting Your Images to Work

Your images can be shared, emailed, put in a slide show, electronically framed, renamed, printed, or used as the portrait on a new $100 bill. Just kidding about that last option, unless you happen to have your own tropical island nation and a printing press. And if so, why haven't you invited me to visit?

 From the Gallery app, tap an image and then tap the Menu icon (shown here). Now choose an option:

- **Details:** You get the nitty gritty: filename and its format, the date and time the photo was taken, and which album it is stored in. If GPS was on, you can see the location. Resolution, whether the camera was held upright or on its side, and the model number of your tablet. It tells you that the flash was off, which is nice to know since the Tab 4 NOOK doesn't have a flash.

✏ **Favorite:** You can tag an image as one of your faves. It won't rename or move the file, but any time you tap the Favorites folder, you'll see only those images upon which you have bestowed this particular honor.

✏ **Slideshow:** Start an automated presentation that goes through every photo in the current folder. You can make the show even more dramatic if you add transition effects and music. You can say for how long you want each picture on the screen.

✏ **Photo Frame:** Add an electronic (but oh-so-elegant) frame around your image. You can also add a note or caption. The edited image is saved in the Photo Frame folder, which is created the first time you use this option.

✏ **Photo Note:** No frame here, but you can write a note and slap it on the image. Tap the pencil icon to write or edit the note.

✏ **Copy to Clipboard:** You can copy and paste any photo into a document.

✏ **Print:** You can send a photo — by USB cable or Wi-Fi connection — to any printer that works with the Galaxy Tab.

✏ **Rename:** Want to give your image a new name? Here's the place.

✏ **Set As:** You can use a picture as the *wallpaper,* or background, on your tablet's Home screen. You can put a picture of a person with that person's contact information, too.

✏ **Buddy Photo Share:** If the image has a person whose face is tagged or identified, this command lets you send the file to that lucky gal or fellow.

✏ **Rotate Left:** Turn the image 90 degrees counterclockwise.

✏ **Rotate Right:** You got this one, right?

✏ **Crop:** Drag the blue frame to resize or use just a part of an image. When you're done, the file is saved for later. Before cropping, save the picture so you have a copy. You might reconsider your crop later.

✏ **Get Directions:** If you have GPS turned on, tapping this option takes you to Google Maps. You can get instructions on how to return to this location by car, public transportation, bicycle, or on foot.

The Get Directions function has many uses, but here are two you might not have thought of: Snap a picture of your car when you park it on the street, or a picture of your hotel in an unfamiliar town. Later, when you need to get your vehicle or make it home to bed, you can ask the Tab 4 NOOK for help. You'll need a Wi-Fi signal to connect to the Google system.

Sharing Your Images

No NOOK tablet is an island, which is a good thing if you want to quickly share your photos with your friends and the world at large. You can send photos several ways, including posting them on social networks and by sending them as email attachments.

In Chapter 5, I explain how to move your photos from your tablet to a desktop or laptop computer; from there you can use fully capable photo editing software and share them in other ways.

From the Gallery you can share by Email, Gmail, Bluetooth, or Wi-Fi Direct. To share an image directly from the Gallery, follow the steps. You must, of course, have an active Wi-Fi connection to share files.

1. **Select a folder and open it.**
2. **Tap the Menu icon and choose Select Item.**

   You can choose one or more images by putting a check mark in the box next to each one.

3. **Tap the Share (forked branch) icon.**
4. **Follow the instructions to share the files with others.**

You can share images right from the Camera app. When you're reviewing a photo, tap the > icon and choose Share.

Shearing Before Sharing: Trimming a Video

The Galaxy Tab 4 NOOK has a basic video editor. You can buy something with a little more oomph as an app from the app stores on your tablet.

If you save the video under a different name from its original, you can keep the full file. This way you can carve up a video into several shorter clips.

To use the tablet's built-in editor, do this:

1. **Open the video file in the Gallery.**
2. **Tap the Trim (scissors) icon.**

   Below your video's large opening scene, you'll see a storyboard-like representation of your full video.

3. **Drag the start bracket to where you want your edited video to begin.**
4. **Move the end bracket to where it should stop. See Figure 12-5.**
5. **Save the video.**

Drag the bracket

Figure 12-5: Move the bracket at the bottom of the panel to adjust the starting and stopping point for a video.

13

Singing and Dancing in the Galaxy

*N*ow, I'm not going to compare the quality of sound you hear from the tiny speakers on the Tab 4 NOOK — a nevertheless amazing pair of devices about the size of the head of a matchstick — with the sound from a much larger system.

And although the LCD screen of the Tab 4 NOOK is beautifully colorful and quite detailed when you're looking at it from a distance of a foot away, it doesn't match the visual thrills of a 90-inch HD screen or the astounding experience at an IMAX theater.

But the Tab 4 NOOK fits in your back pocket or a small purse. And it can be a *source* for audio and video when you connect it to a larger system. This chapter looks at playing items from your well-honed, tasteful collection.

Starting with the Hardware

First of all, there is the internal and external memory, each of which can be used to store files. Since this is, at heart, a computer, those files are *digital* representations of sound and imagery: 0s and 1s that can be converted by the microprocessor into music and movies.

You can get files from almost any source, including the NOOK Shop, Google's Play Music and Movies, Amazon, Apple, YouTube and other web-based sites.

Or you can *stream* audio and video, which means that the material doesn't reside on your tablet but instead arrives from the Internet across a Wi-Fi connection and is immediately played. Music sources include Pandora; many sites provide streaming video of live broadcasting or recorded material.

I discuss Pandora and similar apps online at www.dummies.com/extras/ samsunggalaxytabs.

Speaking of Which . . .

The speakers for your tablet are on the underside. That means the sound may be muffled if you keep your tablet in a case or on a table. I use a tablet stand that holds the device upright and keeps the speakers free and clear to do their thing.

You can get sound from your Tab 4 NOOK all sorts of ways:

- **Headphones.** The 3.5mm headphone jack on the top of the tablet can let you use a headset, which greatly improves the quality of the sound, at least for the one person who can use it. (You can buy a *splitter* so two people can connect headphones to a single tablet, and boy does that ever look geeky. But it works.)

- **Connect to speakers via cable.** You can use the same headphone jack with a cable to connect to an audio system. From there it's sent to larger speakers. I've used my tablet with home stereo systems and was quite pleased with the results.

If you're hooking up to a sound system, the end of the cable that connects to the Tab 4 NOOK must be a 3.5mm stereo plug; you need a plug at the other end to match the system.

As it happens, my car's stereo can use audio through a cable; I bought a male-to-male cable with 3.5mm connectors at each end. You can find cables online if you know exactly what you're looking for. Or, visit a Radio Shack or other such store.

Use your Tab 4 NOOK to take a picture of the connectors on your stereo system. Take the tablet with you to the store.

- **Connect to speakers via Bluetooth.** You can buy *amplified speakers* that communicate with your tablet using Bluetooth radio signals. If you choose this route, I recommend buying a system that includes a sub-woofer, which is an additional speaker devoted entirely to producing deep bass tones.

Jamming Out on Your Tab 4 NOOK

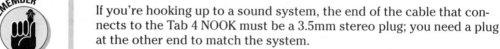

I suppose at some point we're going to drop most of the fancy names for utilities and apps and let them directly tell you what they do. Android gets pretty close to that with its simply titled Music Player.

You'll find it in the Apps collection or, if you've created a shortcut to it, on one of the Home screens. Tap the icon and prepare to groove. (Why do we say *groove* when we mean *enjoy some music?* Because in ancient times, recorded music came on wax and then acetate disks with *grooves* that provided the sound.)

When you open Music Player, you'll see a screen like the one in Figure 13-1. Its tabs are Playlists, Tracks, Albums, Artists, and Folders. Tabs are at the top of the screen; the information varies depending on how you got the music on your tablet and where you stored the files. Tap any tab to see its contents.

Tabs

Shuffle icon

Current track

Play next

Play previous   Pause/Play

Figure 13-1: A glimpse at my exotic music collection. The tabs at the top of the screen are key to organizing your collection.

Choosing what tabs to see

You can change what tabs are shown:

1. **Tap the Menu icon in the upper right.**
2. **Select Settings.**
3. **Tap My Music in the panel on the left.**

   Playlists, Tracks, and Favorites are automatically selected.

4. **Tap a check mark beside the tabs you want to see; deselect a tab you don't want to see.**

   You can see the available categories in Figure 13-2:

   - Playlists
   - Tracks
   - Albums
   - Artists
   - Genres

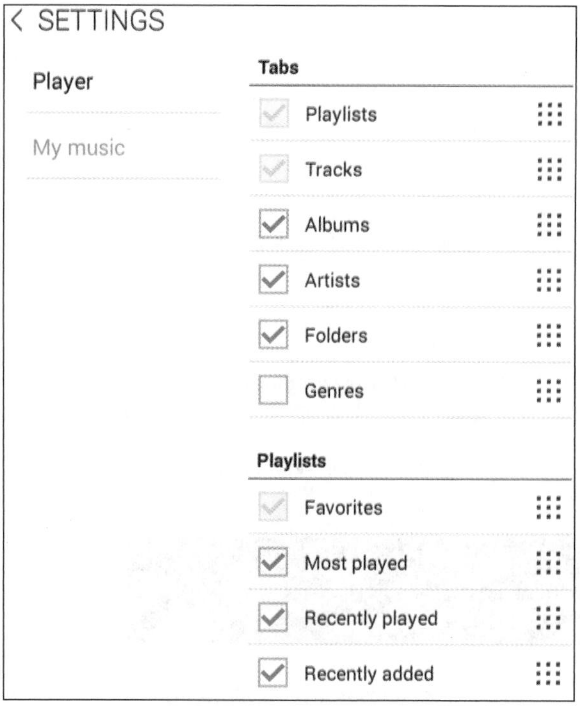

< SETTINGS

Player

My music

Tabs

- ✓ Playlists
- ✓ Tracks
- ✓ Albums
- ✓ Artists
- ✓ Folders
- ☐ Genres

Playlists

- ✓ Favorites
- ✓ Most played
- ✓ Recently played
- ✓ Recently added

Figure 13-2: You can display all or just some of the tabs and playlists associated with your music collection.

Pressing Play

You probably know how to play a track. Okay, if you insist: To play a song, tap any tab or playlist. Then tap the name of a song or artist. Playback is almost instantaneous. No need to wait for the needle to find the right groove, or a CD player to find the chosen track.

- ✔ The current track is at the bottom of the screen scrolling by, and below that you can see a countdown of the time left.
- ✔ Tap Play again to pause the track.
- ✔ Tap Next to skip the current track and move to the next one in your collection; the Previous icon moves the other way through your tracks.
- ✔ Tap the Shuffle icon to skip hither and thon through all the tracks in the current playlist.

If you press the Home key to go to another app, music keeps playing. A Play icon stays in the notification panel (at the top) to remind you that the Music Player is active. Swipe down from the top to see a mini control panel for music. Tapping the X closes the Music Player without you having to go back to the app. See Figure 13-3.

How about a nice piece of music to play while you are reading a book? No problem. Unless you tap Pause or reach the end of your playlist, the Music Player will keep singing to you.

Figure 13-3: The mini Music Player in the notification panel. Pause a track, skip backward or forward, or stop the music.

Tap the Search (magnifying glass) icon to hunt for a track by its name, artist, or album. You can start a song directly from the search results by tapping its name.

Press the Volume key to raise or lower the sound. The end of the switch nearer the Samsung logo on the tablet is + (up); the other end is – (down).

Deleting a song

I almost *never* delete a track of music, because I am a multifaceted guy. As I write these words, I am listening to a 1966 recording of Grace Slick singing "Sally Go Round the Roses" with her original hippie-dippie group The Great Society. Later, I may feel in the mood for Bob Marley, and tonight as I wrap up a long, long day in your service I may close out the night with Rachmaninoff's "Caprice Bohémien." Into which category would you put that particular mix?

But if you insist on removing a track, here's how:

1. **Open the Music Player app.**

2. **Find the track you want to delete.**

   Don't remove a song from a playlist. That just takes it out of the list and does not take it off the tablet.

3. **Press and hold the track in question.**

4. **Tap Delete.**

   Your tablet asks if you're sure.

   A deleted song is gone. If you have another copy on a computer or another tablet, it won't be deleted from there.

5. **Confirm your decision.**

I love this little feature: If you want to use a song from your tablet as the sound for the built-in alarm clock on your tablet, press and hold the title. Tap Select as Alarm Tone. Then confirm.

Creating (smart) playlists

You can create playlists under whatever title and classification you choose.

To create a playlist, do this:

1. **In the My Playlists section, tap the + beside Create Playlist.**

2. **Name your creation.**

3. **Add any track by tapping a check mark next to its name.**

   From now on, tapping the playlist plays only those songs. See Figure 13-4.

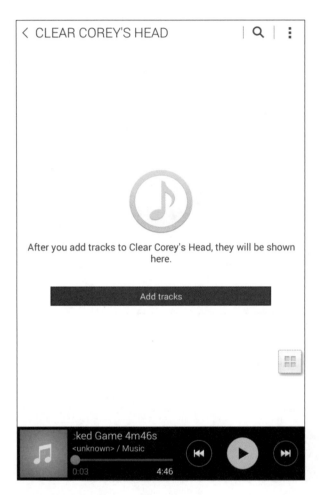

Figure 13-4: After you create a playlist, you can add tracks from your collection. The same track can appear in multiple playlists.

With Music Square, you can let the tablet do the work for you. It analyzes some of your music's sonic qualities. This is very much a touchy-feely utility. It seems to do a good job of distinguishing between a bouncy and happy tune like Van Morrison's "Brown Eyed Girl" (passionate-exciting) and midway between exciting and calm but high on the passionate/joyful scale for Sandy Denny's "Who Knows Where the Time Goes."

To open Music Square, tap the Menu icon in the upper-right corner of the Music Player. Then choose Music Square. See Figure 13-5.

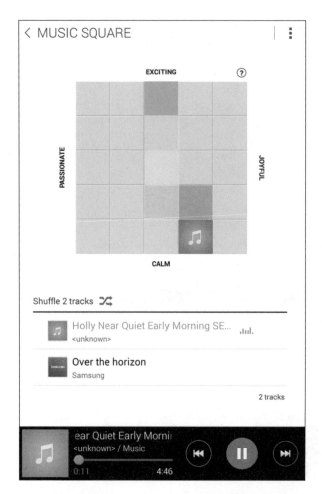

Figure 13-5: Music Square lets you choose music from your collection by tracing a pattern on a grid from calm to exciting, passionate to joyful, and most places in between.

Making the Music Player all Yours

Try this one with your old record player: You can play a track at double speed or half speed. Disappointingly, you cannot, as Joan Baez once sang, "play me backwards."

You have some interesting options in Music Player's settings. To get there, do this:

1. **Tap the Music Player icon.**

2. **Tap the Menu icon in the upper right.**

3. **Choose Settings.**

4. **Tap an option:**

   - **SoundAlive.** You can read more about this option online at www. dummies.com/cheatsheet/samsunggalaxytabs.

   - **Adapt Sound.** Plug in a set of headphones. In a quiet room, tap Start and listen for the very faint tones. They vary in frequency from high to low and shift from ear to ear; tap Yes if you can hear the tone. See Figure 13-6. The Adapt Sound utility plays back a piece of music; you choose between unmodified and adapted versions.

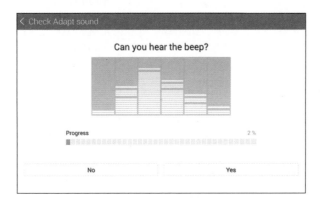

Figure 13-6: Adapt Sound allows you to customize the audio output of your tablet by conducting a hearing test using headphones in a quiet room.

   - **Play Speed.** This speeds up playback or slows it by as much as half. Why would you want to use this feature? Suppose you have a lecture in a file, or a podcast; you can speed up or slow down the track without changing the voice very much.

   - **Music Auto Off.** This timer shuts off the music player after a specified period of time. You can choose from five preset times, or select custom.

   - **Lyrics.** Certain tracks come with lyrics that appear as the track plays. You can turn the feature on or off here.

   - **Smart Volume.** Turn on this feature to automatically adjust each track to an equal level.

Showing Your Own Movies

Although we all aspire to be the next Alfred Hitchcock or Martin Scorsese, I suspect we're all much closer to Alan Smithee. Alan? That was the one and only pseudonym officially recognized by the Directors Guild of America for members who wanted to disown any involvement with their own film.

Of course, your productions don't cost tens or hundreds of millions of dollars. And the magic of digital video means you can point, shoot, and immediately see your work. This chapter deals with video you have made for yourself, using the built-in video camera of the Samsung Galaxy Tab 4 NOOK.

In Chapter 9 of this book, I explain how you can download films from Hollywood, Bollywood, and other woods. When you buy through the NOOK Shop, the Google Play Store, Amazon, Apple, and most other sources, you play the movie using a simple interface that has play, pause, rewind, and fast forward.

Movies that you record with the video camera are stored in the MP4 format. That's not something you have to concern yourself with, except if you want to import another video from a computer or other source; MP4 is the preferred format although the tablet should be able to handle *most* videos encoded in 3GP, WMV, AVI, and a few other formats.

I say the tablet *should* be able to work with other formats because it might balk at files that stray even a tiny bit away from certain formats. You can find some conversion utilities on the Internet that are pretty good at fixing certain deficiencies.

Loading a video

Playing a video that you made with your Tab 4 NOOK is exactly this easy: Find the file, tap the Play icon, sit back (not too far), and watch. It's so easy that Samsung and Google have dotted the Home and the Apps screens with no fewer than four ways to watch a movie.

Using the Gallery to play videos

Here's how to start in the Gallery, which has all your photographs and videos:

1. **In the Apps collection, tap the Gallery icon.**

2. **Tap the folder called Camera.**

   Above the name of the folder you'll see either an icon of a camera or an icon of a tiny strip of film, or both. This lets you know the type of files you'll find inside.

Next to the folder, a number tells you how many files it has: *Camera (2)* means two files.

Photographs are *thumbnails* (small pictures). Video files look similar, but have a large Play icon on them.

3. Tap the Play icon.

The video enlarges to fill the screen.

4. Tap it one more time to start the video.

The first time you watch a video from the Gallery, you may be offered a choice of players: the Video Player or Photos. You can choose one and then tap Always to make that a permanent assignment. If you tap Just Once, you see the same message the next time you play a video from the Gallery. See Figure 13-7.

Figure 13-7: Two apps handle videos you made with the built-in camera: Photos and Video Player. The only difference is that Video Player has a few extra features.

Both Video Player and Photos apps work fine. Both give you access to a basic Trim tool that allows you to choose a starting and ending point for the video. They also have a Details option, which tells you the file's size, resolution, and duration.

Video Player has a few extra options, including Chapter Preview, which gives you a sneak peek at some of the changes in scenery in a lengthy video; it also offers a Share option so you can send the file to YouTube, Picasa, and other services.

Using the Video app

With this app, there's no need to choose a folder.

- ✔ Tap the video's filename or thumbnail.
- ✔ From the Video app, you can tap the Folder icon to search for a specific video.
- ✔ Tap the Search (magnifying glass) icon in the Video app; type a search term.

You can play a video from the Camera and Photos apps.

Managing your videos

You can cut away unwanted parts of a video at its beginning or end using the Trim tool; I explain how in Chapter 12. But to tell you the truth, and I always do, the apps on your Tab 4 NOOK for video aren't all that helpful for anything other than playing them back.

If you want to do some video editing, including cutting, special effects, and sound, transfer the file to a desktop or personal computer and use the software there.

You can share the file with many services and apps, even while you're watching. Tap the Share icon on the screen or do this:

1. **Tap the Play icon to pause.**

2. **Tap the Menu icon.**

3. **Choose Share.**

   Depending on how your tablet is set up and which apps you have, you might be able to send the file by Bluetooth, add it to Dropbox, OneDrive, or another cloud-based storage, or send it as an email or Gmail.

Part V
The Part of Tens

Visit www.dummies.com/extras/samnsunggalaxytab4nook for ten free apps worth checking out.

In this part . . .

- Make the most of apps that are already on your tablet.
- Try some troubleshooting if your tablet throws a tantrum.
- Back up files to protect against disaster.
- Do your best to keep your Tab 4 in tip-top shape.

Ten Apps to Take Advantage Of

*T*his chapter looks at interesting and useful features that automatically come on your tablet. Wade right in and see what else you can do with the Tab 4 NOOK as delivered.

An Alarming Prospect

You can find the Alarm app in the Apps menu; just look for the imaginative icon of an alarm clock. Tap the icon to display its simple charms.

Your alarm will sound even if your tablet is sleeping (just like you). When the alarm sounds, drag the red X outside of the large circle to turn it off. If you turned on the snooze, drag the yellow Zz icon outside the circle to steal a few minutes more. Don't throw your tablet out the window; it could hit someone.

Here's how to manually set an alarm:

1. **Tap the Alarm app icon.**

2. **Tap the + icon in the upper right.**

3. **Tap (or press and hold) the ∧ or ∨ markers to choose hour and then minutes.**

4. **Tap AM or PM.**

5. **Tap one or more days of the week.**

   Those you choose turn green. Tap again to deselect a day.

6. **(Optional) Tap a check mark in Repeat Weekly if you want this alarm to be permanent.**

7. **Tap Alarm Tone to choose the alarm sound.**

   None of them are great works of creativity, and I can't at all figure out why they're given the names they have.

8. **(Optional) Scroll down on the panel to choose from more options:**

   - **Location Alarm.** Is this ever neat: Slide the switch to On. From the Google Maps, tap somewhere or enter its name or address in the bar at the top. When you turn on Location Alarm, the alarm only works when you're there. For example, automatically enable your alarm at work or school.

   - **Snooze.** Get those extra minutes in. You can determine the intervals and the number of times it'll repeat.

   - **Smart Alarm.** Tap a check mark to have the alarm tone or music start at a low volume and slowly increase until you can no longer stand it.

   - **Name.** Keep it clean, because it appears onscreen.

9. **Tap the very small icon of an alarm clock in the right corner of an alarm you have created to turn it on.**

   It changes to green when enabled. Tap it again to disable it.

10. **You're done setting up an alarm, but *you have to set it or it won't trigger.***

    To get rid of an alarm, press and hold on its face in the Alarm app. Then tap the trash can icon that appears in the upper right corner of the screen.

Planning Your Day with the Calendar

If you use the same Google account on your tablet and your smartphone and your laptop, they'll be synced. You can change your calendar on any device, but *syncing* depends on an Internet connection. If you're not online at the moment, then the device syncs the first chance it gets.

To connect an Outlook.com calendar to your Android calendar, you must download a free app called Outlook. I know this may be confusing, but the Microsoft app is offered for free from the Google Play Store.

I have two points to make about the interconnectivity of devices with the Calendar on your Tab 4 NOOK:

- You can make it work. (I use it daily.)

- You may need the promised free help of Samsung, Google, Barnes & Noble, Microsoft, and that smart-aleck kid down the block to set everything up to your liking. Or you may figure it out on your own. There are simply too many combinations for me to outline them all here.

You can add an event several ways. Here's one that you do from the Calendar app on the Tab 4 NOOK:

1. **Tap the day for the event.**

2. **Tap the + icon.**

3. **Add a title or subject for the event.**

4. **Tap in the From and then the To fields to choose a date from the onscreen calendar.**

5. **Select the beginning and then ending time for the event.**

   You can add a special icon and make the event repeat daily, weekly, monthly, or on another schedule. You can get a reminder at a specified time before the event or at the very moment it's supposed to happen.

Reminders display across all devices that are synced to the same calendar. While writing this book on a desktop computer, I had my brand-new Tab 4 NOOK to the left of the computer and my smartphone on the right. All three chirped at me to remind me to pick up my wife from work; a good thing, too, because she has come to expect such superior service from me.

Five tabs are at the top of the calendar: Year, Month, Week, Day, and Agenda. Tap one to change your view. Tap an event to see a full description.

If you're syncing events from several calendars onto your Tab 4 NOOK, each will have a different color bar alongside.

1. **Tap the Settings (gear) icon in the upper right.**

2. **Tap Calendars.**

3. **Turn on (or off) the sync to see different calendars and to see their color code.**

Get Offa My Clouds

The Tab 4 NOOK comes with two free cloud-based storage options: Dropbox and Drive. Those options are helpful for tablet users when you use your tablet as an adjunct to your desktop computer.

For example, I make copies of my works in progress, as well as important reference documents, and store them in the cloud (meaning, I save copies on Dropbox or Drive). And then, if I unexpectedly need to use something when I'm traveling, I sign in to the storage and download the file.

Give 'em a Hancom

Your tablet has an app called Hancom Office, which includes Hanword, Hancell, and Hanshow. Don't expect to write the Great American Novel on your Tab 4 NOOK. Hanword and Hancell allow, with a bit of difficulty, the editing of Word and Excel documents. Hanshow can use PowerPoint documents but without most of the fancy animations, transitions, and sound effects that I use in my lectures around the world.

As Chief Brody more or less said to the shark-hunter Quint in *Jaws:* You're going to need a bigger screen and keyboard.

You can also set up cloud storage to store copies of all photos you take with your tablet; you can later delete them from your tablet to save space and then download them from the cloud to your desktop or laptop computer.

Checking Your Latitude

Use the Maps app to search for restaurants, hotels, hospitals, and just about anything else in this wide world.

Lots of things to remember about GPS:

- ✓ If you want to know where you are, you must turn on the GPS. You can do so by tapping the Settings (gear) icon.

- ✓ To see if it's on, swipe down from the top of the screen to bring up the notification panel and check for the icon.

- ✓ If you're asked to allow the system to use Wi-Fi systems to fine-tune its ability to find itself, I recommend doing that.

- ✓ You need an active Wi-Fi connection to see a Google map of where you are, and to plot a course. If you connect to the Internet using Wi-Fi and get the necessary map, you can go off Wi-Fi and still see the last map displayed, which will be some help.

The Google Maps app doesn't follow the same layout as most of the Android, Samsung, or NOOK screens. Keep these tips in mind:

- ✓ The Menu icon is in the upper-left corner. Before you head out on the road, spend some time checking out the Help and Tips and Tricks sections.

- ✓ Tapping the tiny compass rose icon (lower right) takes you back to your current location from anywhere else you may have virtually traveled.

- ✓ Save maps to your tablet for when you're not connected to the Internet.

I've already put the route I plan to take on a trip from Sorrento, Italy to the ancient Greek settlement of Paestum below Salerno. It's only 100 kilometers (about 62 miles), but the first ten are along the Sorrentine coastline and I'm going to need all the help I can get: Tab 4 NOOK with the Maps app, my smartphone with a data stream, a GPS, and my wife screaming in terror at each sharp bend in the road. Wish me luck: My route is in Figure 14-1 and the step-by-step instructions are a tap away.

Menu icon

GPS is on

Compass rose icon

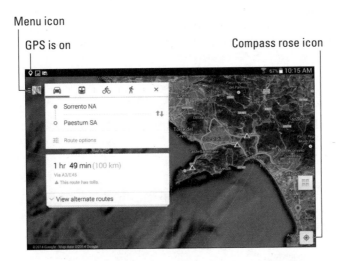

Figure 14-1: You can type or speak to the Maps app. My itinerary is from Sorrento (in the Italian province of Napoli) to Paestum (in Salerno).

Have the Tuna Eat the Mayo: Taking a Memo

The Memo app lets you make short notes, but it ties into other features on your tablet. For example, you can send a memo by email, Gmail, Wi-Fi Direct, Bluetooth, Drive, Dropbox, and more. Tap the microphone in the upper-left corner of the memo to record your voice or any other audio to the message.

And if you have what is commonly referred to as "fat fingers," tap the larger microphone icon on the keyboard to dictate your memo. You can edit or change any document you create.

Popcorn, Soda Pop, and Netflix

If you already have a Netflix account for your TV, you can access it from your Tab 4 NOOK. (At the moment, you can't get popcorn and soda streamed to your tablet via Wi-Fi.) If not, you can set up an account right here to stream television series, current movies, and classics.

One key point: Make sure you have a strong, fast Wi-Fi signal for streaming video. A weak, slow signal will remind some of you of the days before cable, when a distant broadcast channel looked like it was being broadcast through a snowstorm. Swipe down from the top to see the strength in the notification panel.

Editing Photos Without the Shop

People sometimes look at one of my photos with admiration, and then ask me which camera and lens I use. Not to call myself Picasso, but the question is somewhat as if someone had asked the master which brand of paint or charcoal he used.

The Galaxy Tab 4 NOOK camera is very basic, but it's nevertheless a camera, and the photographer's eye matters most. But even the best photographer needs to go into the darkroom — or now, the digital darkroom — to adjust brightness or contrast. The Photos app, from Google, does all that and so much more.

Editing with the Photos app

Display an image by tapping the small version. Then tap the Edit (pen) icon at the lower left.

Controls are at the bottom of the screen. See Figure 14-2 for a tour:

- **Auto.** Experiment with two settings: Normal and High. An icon at the top center lets you flash between the enhanced and original versions. To apply the settings, tap the check mark; to cancel the effect, press X.

- **Crop.** Drag a handle at the corner, top, or bottom to crop the image. The section of the image that will be removed gets dark. When finished, tap the check mark to accept or tap the X to abandon the crop.

- **Rotate.** You can rotate the central part of the image as much as 45 degrees left or right.

Figure 14-2: Here are some of the edit tools available in Photos. I took this photo of a Gnawa musician within the Kasbah at Rabat, Morocco.

✔ **Looks.** Tap the rainbow icon centered above the image to go back and forth between the adjusted and original file.

✔ **Tune.** Touch and hold anywhere in the image; swipe down to display a menu that offers brightness, contrast, saturation, shadows, and warmth. Select one and move your finger off the menu. Then touch the image and swipe left or right to apply one of the adjustments on a scale from -100 to +100. The 0 point represents the unadjusted image.

✔ **Selective.** This control — not well designed in the current edition of the app — allows you to select an advanced effect and apply it to *parts* of the image. I suggest waiting for the next release of this app before wasting time here.

✔ **Details.** Choose between two types of image sharpening. Touch and hold anywhere in the image; then swipe down to show the menu. Select a tool, and then swipe left or right to apply it.

Slide the tools at the bottom of the image to the left to fully display eight more options. They include Vintage, Drama, Black & White, Retrolux, Center Focus, Tilt Shift, and Frames.

Adjustments you make using Photos can be cumulative; you can move from effect to effect and keep adding changes. When you finally save your image, it's a copy of the original; the unedited version is kept, too. See Figure 14-3.

Edit   Share   Delete

Figure 14-3: For this image, from the slaver island of Gorée in Dakar, Senegal, I adjusted contrast and then applied an orange filter to enhance the contrast.

Sharing and archiving

You can share any image from the Photos app by tapping the Share (two-pronged) icon at the bottom of the picture.

A quick trip into Settings lets you save every photo you take with the Tab 4 NOOK to your Google+ account. And there, the cloud has another, more powerful editor called Auto Enhance. For auto backup, tap the Menu icon in the upper right and then turn on the option.

Talking to Your Tab 4 NOOK

How about teaching your tablet to respond to your questions? The Tab 4 NOOK has two personal audio servants (a term I just made up; feel free to use it any time you want).

The Google system is the more full-featured, hobbled mostly by its uninspired name: Voice Search. It can answer questions like the one I asked: "Where is the nearest post office?" See Figure 14-4.

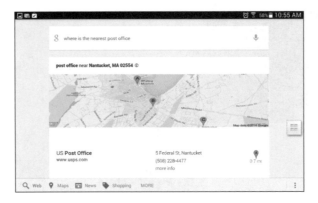

Figure 14-4: Voice Search can combine the Google search engine with Google Maps. I asked for the nearest post office.

Use Voice Search to issue a command.

As I worked on this chapter, I knew that I had a conference call scheduled with my favorite editor. I told Voice Search, "Set an alarm for 11:55 a.m. today for my telephone conference call." And it did just that; remember the manual process for alarms I discuss earlier in this very same chapter? This is much more fun, and quicker.

Samsung's version of voice recognition is called S Voice, and it's quite capable as well. You can ask, "Will it rain tonight?" or command it to "Turn on Wi-Fi" or "Show me the calculator" or "Play music." I also like the pleasant tone and polite discourse of S Voice. She said it was nice to meet me, and then took on an almost impossible assignment with computer-generated charm.

Here's a slightly hidden trick: You can open S Voice by double-pressing the Home key. Tap the Menu icon for other voice settings.

My Tube or YouTube

Tap the YouTube icon for a quick connection to a seemingly endless supply of videos of kittens who think they're trapped in a grocery bag. See Figure 14-5.

You'll also find very amateur films of parties and celebrations for people you don't know and probably would never want to meet. But I also find an occasional gem in historical footage or old movies. And if you want to see a visual demonstration on how to unclog a bathroom drain or make the perfect buttermilk biscuit, you'll find it here as well.

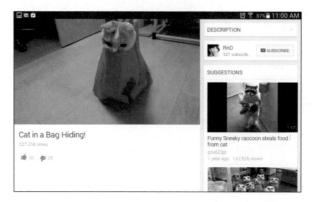

Figure 14-5: You perhaps thought I was kidding about the cat in a grocery bag? Even more amazing, 327,257 people watched before I did. Is this wonderful, or not?

And you can upload your own video for the world to see, right from your Tab 4 NOOK. Use the YouTube app or tap the Share icon in the Gallery where your videos are stored. Your Google account ties into a YouTube account.

Using Your Most Expensive Calculator

Funnily enough, the first truly electronic device that many people ever touched — way back in the 1960s — was a calculator. They were state-of-the-art and the nerdiest of the nerds wore them in belt holsters in a pathetic attempt to show how with-it they were. I think I still have my holster in a drawer somewhere.

Today, you just tap the Calculator icon in the Apps menu. Hold your tablet in portrait mode (taller than wide) and you'll see a simple calculator with basic mathematical operators. Then, you can turn your tablet sideways either direction (wider than tall) to see the scientific calculator with all of those symbols you learned about in high school and have long since forgotten.

15

Ten Steps to Maintaining the Galaxy

....

....

*Y*ou are now a guardian of the Galaxy. This exalted role, straight out of the pages of superhero comics, comes with some awesome and heavy responsibilities.

Treat the Battery with Respect

Here is how to get the most life from your tablet's battery:

- ✔ Allow it to fully charge when you can, and then unplug it.
- ✔ Don't leave it attached to the charger constantly.
- ✔ Don't let the battery reach empty. It could damage it.

If your battery can't hold a charge when turned off for the night, or seems to use up its power much quicker than usual, during that first year contact Barnes & Noble or bring the device into one of the stores and insist on a repair. Don't wait for the 365th day, either; they might start counting down from the day it was shipped rather than the day you received the tablet.

And if the battery starts to fail *after* one year, get a price for installation of a replacement and then consider whether it makes sense to pay the fee. Sad to say, many high-tech devices are not worth repairing.

It's normal for the tablet and battery to be warm during use and recharging. If it starts getting *hot,* and by that I mean painful to the touch or capable of frying an egg, turn it off and unplug it from the AC adapter. Then contact Barnes & Noble and politely insist they deal with a potential fire hazard.

Protect the Charger, Too

Here are some suggestions about how to treat the charger properly:

- ✔ If possible, don't plug it directly into a wall socket. Instead, attach it to a power strip that has a surge protector.
- ✔ If a charger starts to go beyond warm to very hot, unplug it and consult with Barnes & Noble.

- ✔ Buy a second charger. Make sure it's a Samsung brand charger, and that it matches exactly the specifications of the original: 5 volts DC at 1 amp output. Put the second charger in your travel kit or your car, whichever makes sense. The tablet charger is the same as is used on many (but not all) Samsung tablets and smartphones. Check the specifications (see above) to see if you can repurpose one you already have.

Don't Let the Galaxy Fall to Earth

Here are a couple of ways you can reduce the chances:

- ✔ Buy a protective case or tablet stand (or both). The case will protect against most sharp objects. A tablet stand will hold the device at an angle that makes it easier to see while seated.
- ✔ While the AC adapter is connected to the tablet, be aware of where the cable runs. Don't accidentally pull your tablet to the floor.
- ✔ Take care when moving your tablet from place to place.

Safeguard the Connector

Laptop and tablet repair companies report that broken connectors are the most common issue they have to deal with. When the tablet has a plug stuck into the port at the bottom (where the AC adapter attaches), it's quite vulnerable to damage. Also try to keep the headphone jack at the top clean; don't let dirt or sand or melted chocolate enter there.

I suggest using a tablet stand, but be extra careful if the connector is attached while the tablet's in the stand.

Don't Bring Your Own Beverage

Aside from dropping your tablet from a great height or allowing a school bus to run over it, the other major threat to a piece of electronics is a spill: water, soda, coffee, Chardonnay, or anything else.

Keep a Clean Screen

Here's how to keep a clean screen:

- ✔ Wash your hands from time to time. Then dry them.
- ✔ Clean the screen with a *dry* soft cloth. A clean piece of cotton fabric works well.
- ✔ I said use a *dry* cloth. Never, ever use any chemicals to clean the screen — especially alcohol, ammonia, or solvents.
- ✔ If keeping the screen clean becomes a serious problem, consider buying a screen protector.

Don't Point at the Display

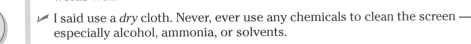

The sharpest thing to touch your screen should be your finger.

- ✔ Don't try to scratch a command.
- ✔ Don't use a pen or other sharp implement on your tablet.
- ✔ Don't use a stylus. Samsung offers a smartphone series called the Galaxy Note, which uses a special stylus for writing. Your Galaxy Tab 4 NOOK *isn't* the same device.

Watch for the Misplaced Key

Just my opinion here, but I find the Power/Lock key's placement one of the relatively few design mistakes for the hardware. The key is much too easy to press. I've been working almost constantly with the Tab 4 NOOK for several weeks and I've accidentally locked the screen and even turned off the tablet more times than I can remember.

There's no solution other than to teach yourself key awareness (and hope that Samsung engineers will do a bit of ergonomic testing before the next model is released).

Clean Up the Memory

Removing unnecessary apps can give you space. Are there apps that you've decided are no use to you? Do you avoid any apps because they cause problems?

Here's how to remove downloaded apps:

1. **Pull down the notification panel from the top of the screen.**
2. **Tap the Settings (gear) icon and choose the General tab.**
3. **Tap the Application manager in the left panel.**
4. **Slide the scrolling categories to select Downloaded.**
5. **Tap the app name.**
6. **Tap Uninstall to delete the app.**

Removing downloads, photos, videos, and text files you no longer need can help free up space, too:

- Attach the USB cable to the tablet and then to a desktop or laptop PC. Look on your Tab 4 NOOK from the larger computer's File Explorer or Finder. Consider creating a temporary or permanent storage folder on your computer to hold files that you take off the tablet; you could reinstall them if needed.

- Open apps that create or manage files and delete files you don't need.

- Use a file manager app on your tablet to delete unneeded documents, or move them from device memory to the microSDHC card.

Back Up Your Data

I hate to end this chapter on a down note, but I have three important pieces of advice: back up, back up, and back up. You don't want to lose your photos, videos, text files, and other documents.

Here's how:

✔ Use one of the cloud backup services to upload copies of your files. Keep them in sync so that changes you make are reflected in the stored version. The Tab 4 NOOK comes with a Dropbox account and a Google Drive account; you can also add a OneDrive account from the Play Store. In their basic form, they're all free; there's no reason not to use one or all.

✔ Connect your tablet to a desktop or laptop PC using the USB cable from time to time and copy important tablet files to your computer.

Your Google account automatically backs up Gmail and other googly material to that company's servers. What about books, videos, and music? In most cases, you can reinstall what you bought on a new device if you use the same account information. Consult the shops and keep on the lookout for any changes to terms and conditions.

16

Ten Galaxy Tips and Tricks

*Y*ou may run into some bumps along the way with your tablet. I'm here to help.

Your Tab 4 NOOK Won't Turn On

Is the battery completely empty? Use the AC adapter and give your Tab 4 NOOK at least an hour. If the device still fails to turn on after a recharge, it's time to call in the troops: Call the NOOK center at 800-843-2665, use the online chat from www.nook.com, or visit a Barnes & Noble store. Go there first. However, Samsung may be able to help. Visit their website or call 800-726-7864 if you think you're dealing with a hardware problem not of your own making.

You can't use the USB cable and a computer port to charge and use the tablet at the same time; the tablet must be off.

Your Tab 4 NOOK Won't Turn Off

Try the following:

1. **Unplug the USB cable from the AC adapter (if it's attached to your tablet).**

2. **Remove any device connected to the headphone jack.**

3. **Press and hold the Power/Lock key for 15 to 20 seconds.**

4. **If the tablet turns off: Wait a few seconds, turn it on, and check its operation. Then try turning it off in the usual manner.**

   If the tablet doesn't turn off: It's time to try a reset. I discuss that in a moment.

   If the reset doesn't fix the problem, do nothing else. Do not pass Go. Call NOOK customer care for assistance.

Your Tablet Is a Power Vampire

What can you do? Turn down its screen brightness. Get in the habit of pressing the Power/Lock key anytime you walk away from the tablet for a few minutes. Turn on the power saving mode.

Extend Your Warranty

Many credit cards offer added protection for devices that you've bought with those pieces of magic plastic. For example, American Express Extended Warranty automatically doubles the warranty protection for most devices — including tablets — for as much as one year. Contact customer service for any credit cards you own to see if this is included.

My recommendation: Always use credit cards with warranty protection when you buy electronic devices.

Find the Hidden Task Manager

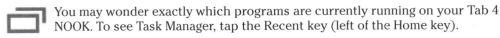

You may wonder exactly which programs are currently running on your Tab 4 NOOK. To see Task Manager, tap the Recent key (left of the Home key).

You'll see these categories: Active Applications, Downloaded, RAM Manager — if you get the feeling that your tablet is slogging through molasses instead of skating across clear ice, check here — and Storage.

The Clear Cache option can sometimes clean up things after a crash or slowdown.

Visit Android System Recovery

Deeply hidden — and not mentioned in the NOOK manual or the Samsung manual or in the daily SPAM mail you receive offering you millions of dollars in unclaimed lottery winnings — is a secret control panel for Android.

Now, if you want, go ahead and look at this screen. But *please* read all of the instructions fully and don't make any sudden movements because you could end up making things much worse. Ready? Really? Okay:

1. **Turn off your tablet and let it catch its breath for a second or two.**

   Crack your knuckles and stretch your fingers.

2. **Hold the tablet in your *left hand* in portrait mode (taller than wide) with the Samsung label at the top.**

3. **Rest your left pointer finger on the Power/Lock key.**

4. **Rest your right thumb on the Home key.**

5. **Rest your right pointer finger on the Volume + (up) key.**

6. **Now press and hold all three keys at the same time.**

7. **When the Samsung logo appears, let go of all three keys.**

   A few seconds later you will find yourself in the deep, dark recesses of the Android system recovery screen. The highlighted line on the screen will read Reboot System Now.

8. ***Read this carefully:* Use the Volume key to move the highlight bar. Go down four steps, to Wipe Cache Partition.**

   Don't go anywhere else. (Especially stay away from Wipe Data/Factory Reset.)

9. **With Wipe Cache Partition highlighted, press the Power/Lock key.**

   The little Android guy on the screen will hop, and a message reports that the cache has been *wiped,* which means cleared away.

10. **Make sure that Reboot System Now is highlighted. Check again, please.**

11. **Press the Power/Lock key to restart your tablet.**

    Welcome to the super-secret Android geek club.

Troubleshoot Apps

Most apps work as advertised. Some don't. One way to see if one of your added apps is causing problems is to reboot your tablet into the somewhat secret Safe Mode.

Bad app. Bad app!

Quick story: I took my fancy smartphone into a company store run by my cellular provider to ask about a problem I was having. A nice young man there brought my phone to his desk and plugged in a connector to a computer. He then loaded an app on my phone which ran diagnostics. "Nothing wrong with your phone," he said. But when I continued on my way home, I could watch the battery level draining, like water down the drain. When I called the company (on another phone) we determined that the *app* their own representative had loaded onto my phone wasn't authorized and was chewing through electrons like a teenager at an all-you-can-eat buffet. I removed the app.

Turning On Safe Mode

Here's how to turn on your tablet in Safe Mode:

1. **Turn off your Tab 4 NOOK.**

2. **Press and hold the Power/Lock key for one or two seconds to turn it on.**

3. **When the Samsung logo displays, press and hold the Volume – (down) key until the NOOK logo appears.**

4. **Let go of the Volume key.**

   The unlock screen shows up, and you'll see Safe Mode in the lower left. Test your Tab 4 NOOK. If all seems well, your next step is to figure out which app is causing the problem.

Turning Off Safe Mode

Safe Mode is turned off when you shut down and restart your tablet. Here's a quick route to that:

1. **Press and hold the Power/Lock key for one or two seconds.**

2. **Tap Restart.**

Troubleshooting apps

Try to work backward from the most recent app you installed or updated. What's changed since the last time the tablet was working properly?

Uninstall (take off) apps or updates using the Application manager. Here's how:

1. **Pull down from the top to display the notification panel.**

2. **Tap the Settings (gear) icon and choose the General tab.**

3. **Tap the Application manager from the panel on the left side.**

4. **Swipe left or right near the top to display the Downloaded tab.**

5. **Tap the app you want to uninstall.**

6. **Tap Uninstall.**

It may take a while, but I suggest uninstalling one app at a time and restarting the tablet each time. You can't uninstall apps that came preloaded on your tablet.

Do a Soft Reset

A *soft reset* tells the device to forget any recent commands or data. It doesn't erase any of your books, documents, or configuration settings. To soft reset, do this:

1. **Press and hold the Power/Lock key for 20 seconds, then release the key.**

2. **Press the Power/Lock key again for 3 seconds to turn on your tablet.**

Go to Super-Secret Developer Mode

Developer Options has settings usually reserved for people who are writing apps or developing software.

If you turn on Developer Options, there's no easy going back. The Developer Options panel is always on the General tab. As long as you keep Developer Options in the Off position, no changes will be made to your operating system. The only way to remove the Developer Options panel is to perform a factory reset. Proceed at your own risk.

Here's how to load the mode:

1. **Pull down the notification panel from the top of the screen.**

2. **Tap the Settings (gear) icon and choose the General tab.**

3. **In the left panel, scroll up to and tap About Device.**

4. **In the right panel, find Build Number.**

   It should be grayed out.

5. **Tap Build Number not once, not twice, but *seven* times.**

   Seven as in seven dwarves, seven brides for seven brothers, seven sleepers.

6. **Move the slide switch at the top of the screen to the left or gray position.**

   Any changes you might have made are *disabled.*

Perform a Factory Reset

A *factory reset* deletes all your settings, including your NOOK account, Google account, Samsung account, and any others you have registered. It also *permanently* removes all files, including books, movies, music, text, and photos.

You might consider performing the dire act known as a factory reset for two reasons:

- All other attempts at fixing an operating system or app problem have failed and you're willing to start over. Completely.
- You want to sell or give your Samsung Galaxy Tab 4 NOOK to someone and you want to remove all traces of passwords, account names, photos, and anything else you've added to the device.

Here are the steps:

1. **Pull down the notification panel from the top of the screen.**

2. **Tap the Settings (gear) icon and choose the General tab.**

3. **In the left panel, tap Backup and Restore.**

4. **In the right panel, tap Factory Data Reset.**

   Really? Are you sure?

5. **Tap Reset Device.**

Index

About the Author

Corey Sandler has lived a life (thus far) probably worthy of two or three "About the Author" entries. He holds degrees in journalism and psychology from Syracuse University back in the days when writers pecked away on typewriters and publishers hired squadrons of monks to hand-letter and illustrate parchment books. Well, at least the first part is true.

As an undergraduate and graduate student he also played around with a gigantic IBM mainframe computer, writing software programs that performed advanced assignments like figuring batting averages for the newborn New York Mets and calculating the proper tip for pizza delivery. He went on to work for daily newspapers in Ohio and New York, covering local and then national politics before joining The Associated Press as a newsman.

When the first personal computers were introduced, Corey managed to switch off the portion of his brain devoted to baseball, pizza tips, and politics and turn back on his interest in computers. He became the first Executive Editor of *PC Magazine* in 1983 and wrote about and directed the coverage of the birth of personal computer industry, the Internet, and microwaveable pizza.

About 25 years ago he decided to try his hand at books. Since then he has written more than 200 titles on computers . . . and travel, business, and sports.

When he began writing about computers, the devices came with ten-pound "technical manuals" typed by engineers and programmers. Today, tablets and other technology often come with no instruction books at all; not that they don't need them, but it seems manufacturers have decided not to even bother.

That's a good thing, at least for those of us who make a nice living translating mysterious onscreen menus and hidden features into language readers can actually use. We call them *books*.

Corey lives with his lovely wife on the lovely island of Nantucket, 30 miles off the coast of Cape Cod in Massachusetts. Their two children, no longer troublesome laptops, have begun their own lives on the mainland. About half the year, Corey travels the world as a destination lecturer for one of the most luxurious cruise lines in the world. (Someone has to do it.) You can vicariously travel along at www.blog.sandlerbooks.com.

Back on his island, the winds may howl and the seas may rage, but these days a cable delivers high-speed Internet right to the computer over in the corner — the one he's using to write these words right now.

Dedication

What? Another heartfelt dedication to Janice, my life partner, muse, and first reader? You bet.

Author's Acknowledgments

I would like to thank fellow traveler (metaphorically speaking) Tonya Maddox Cupp, who polished my prose with professionalism. And Katie Mohr of Wiley, my faithful patron. Once again, they are my publishing all-stars.

Publisher's Acknowledgments

Senior Acquisitions Editor: Katie Mohr

Project Editor: Tonya Maddox Cupp

Editorial Assistant: Claire Johnson

Sr. Editorial Assistant: Cherie Case

Project Coordinator: Patrick Redmond

Project Manager: Mary Corder

Cover Image: ©iStock.com/Giorgio Magini

pple & Mac

ad For Dummies,
th Edition
78-1-118-72306-7

hone For Dummies,
th Edition
78-1-118-69083-3

lacs All-in-One
or Dummies, 4th Edition
78-1-118-82210-4

S X Mavericks
or Dummies
78-1-118-69188-5

logging & Social Media

acebook For Dummies,
th Edition
78-1-118-63312-0

ocial Media Engagement
or Dummies
78-1-118-53019-1

VordPress For Dummies,
th Edition
78-1-118-79161-5

Business

tock Investing
or Dummies, 4th Edition
978-1-118-37678-2

nvesting For Dummies,
5th Edition
978-0-470-90545-6

Personal Finance
For Dummies, 7th Edition
978-1-118-11785-9

QuickBooks 2014
For Dummies
978-1-118-72005-9

Small Business Marketing
Kit For Dummies,
3rd Edition
978-1-118-31183-7

Careers

Job Interviews
For Dummies, 4th Edition
978-1-118-11290-8

Job Searching with Social
Media For Dummies,
2nd Edition
978-1-118-67856-5

Personal Branding
For Dummies
978-1-118-11792-7

Resumes For Dummies,
6th Edition
978-0-470-87361-8

Starting an Etsy Business
For Dummies, 2nd Edition
978-1-118-59024-9

Diet & Nutrition

Belly Fat Diet For Dummies
978-1-118-34585-6

Mediterranean Diet
For Dummies
978-1-118-71525-3

Nutrition For Dummies,
5th Edition
978-0-470-93231-5

Digital Photography

Digital SLR Photography
All-in-One For Dummies,
2nd Edition
978-1-118-59082-9

Digital SLR Video &
Filmmaking For Dummies
978-1-118-36598-4

Photoshop Elements 12
For Dummies
978-1-118-72714-0

Gardening

Herb Gardening
For Dummies, 2nd Edition
978-0-470-61778-6

Gardening with Free-Range
Chickens For Dummies
978-1-118-54754-0

Health

Boosting Your Immunity
For Dummies
978-1-118-40200-9

Diabetes For Dummies,
4th Edition
978-1-118-29447-5

Living Paleo For Dummies
978-1-118-29405-5

Big Data

Big Data For Dummies
978-1-118-50422-2

Data Visualization
For Dummies
978-1-118-50289-1

Hadoop For Dummies
978-1-118-60755-8

Language & Foreign Language

500 Spanish Verbs
For Dummies
978-1-118-02382-2

English Grammar
For Dummies, 2nd Edition
978-0-470-54664-2

French All-in-One
For Dummies
978-1-118-22815-9

German Essentials
For Dummies
978-1-118-18422-6

Italian For Dummies,
2nd Edition
978-1-118-00465-4

Available in print and e-book formats.

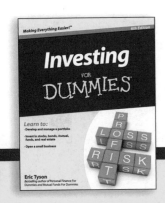

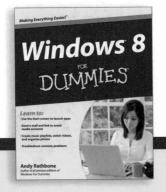

Available wherever books are sold. **For more information or to order direct visit www.dummies.com**

Math & Science

Algebra I For Dummies, 2nd Edition
978-0-470-55964-2

Anatomy and Physiology For Dummies, 2nd Edition
978-0-470-92326-9

Astronomy For Dummies, 3rd Edition
978-1-118-37697-3

Biology For Dummies, 2nd Edition
978-0-470-59875-7

Chemistry For Dummies, 2nd Edition
978-1-118-00730-3

1001 Algebra II Practice Problems For Dummies
978-1-118-44662-1

Microsoft Office

Excel 2013 For Dummies
978-1-118-51012-4

Office 2013 All-in-One For Dummies
978-1-118-51636-2

PowerPoint 2013 For Dummies
978-1-118-50253-2

Word 2013 For Dummies
978-1-118-49123-2

Music

Blues Harmonica For Dummies
978-1-118-25269-7

Guitar For Dummies, 3rd Edition
978-1-118-11554-1

iPod & iTunes For Dummies, 10th Edition
978-1-118-50864-0

Programming

Beginning Programming with C For Dummies
978-1-118-73763-7

Excel VBA Programming For Dummies, 3rd Edition
978-1-118-49037-2

Java For Dummies, 6th Edition
978-1-118-40780-6

Religion & Inspiration

The Bible For Dummies
978-0-7645-5296-0

Buddhism For Dummies, 2nd Edition
978-1-118-02379-2

Catholicism For Dummies, 2nd Edition
978-1-118-07778-8

Self-Help & Relationships

Beating Sugar Addiction For Dummies
978-1-118-54645-1

Meditation For Dummies, 3rd Edition
978-1-118-29144-3

Seniors

Laptops For Seniors For Dummies, 3rd Edition
978-1-118-71105-7

Computers For Seniors For Dummies, 3rd Edition
978-1-118-11553-4

iPad For Seniors For Dummies, 6th Edition
978-1-118-72826-0

Social Security For Dummies
978-1-118-20573-0

Smartphones & Tablets

Android Phones For Dummies, 2nd Edition
978-1-118-72030-1

Nexus Tablets For Dummies
978-1-118-77243-0

Samsung Galaxy S 4 For Dummies
978-1-118-64222-1

Samsung Galaxy Tabs For Dummies
978-1-118-77294-2

Test Prep

ACT For Dummies, 5th Edition
978-1-118-01259-8

ASVAB For Dummies, 3rd Edition
978-0-470-63760-9

GRE For Dummies, 7th Edition
978-0-470-88921-3

Officer Candidate Tests For Dummies
978-0-470-59876-4

Physician's Assistant Exam For Dummies
978-1-118-11556-5

Series 7 Exam For Dummies
978-0-470-09932-2

Windows 8

Windows 8.1 All-in-One For Dummies
978-1-118-82087-2

Windows 8.1 For Dummies
978-1-118-82121-3

Windows 8.1 For Dummies, Book + DVD Bundle
978-1-118-82107-7

e Available in print and e-book formats.

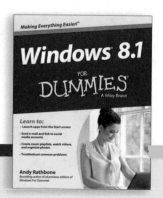

Available wherever books are sold. **For more information or to order direct visit www.dummies.com**

Take Dummies with you everywhere you go!

Whether you are excited about e-books, want more from the web, must have your mobile apps, or are swept up in social media, Dummies makes everything easier.

Leverage the Power

For Dummies is the global leader in the reference category and one of the most trusted and highly regarded brands in the world. No longer just focused on books, customers now have access to the For Dummies content they need in the format they want. Let us help you develop a solution that will fit your brand and help you connect with your customers.

Advertising & Sponsorships

Connect with an engaged audience on a powerful multimedia site, and position your message alongside expert how-to content.

Targeted ads • Video • Email marketing • Microsites • Sweepstakes sponsorship

21 Million Monthly Page Views & 13 Million Unique Visitors

# of For Dummies

Custom Publishing

Reach a global audience in any language by creating a solution that will differentiate you from competitors, amplify your message, and encourage customers to make a buying decision.

Apps • Books • eBooks • Video • Audio • Webinars

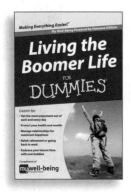

Brand Licensing & Content

Leverage the strength of the world's most popular reference brand to reach new audiences and channels of distribution.

For more information, visit www.Dummies.com/biz

Dummies products make life easier!

- DIY
- Consumer Electronics
- Crafts
- Software
- Cookware
- Hobbies
- Videos
- Music
- Games
- and More!

For more information, go to **Dummies.com** and search the store by category.

FOR
DUMMIES

A Wiley Brand